GW00771466

The Garden Grows Cookbook

Spring
summer
autumn
winter

The Garden Grows Cookbook

An ecological guide to the selection and preparation of food

Recipes by Eva Lambert
Text by Tony Lambert

Illustrated by
Carina MacDonald and Eva Lambert

WILDWOOD HOUSE LONDON

First published 1978

Wildwood House Ltd
29 King Street
London WC2E 8JD

ISBN Hardback 0 7045 0339 5
Paperback 0 7045 0320 4

Typeset by Supreme Litho Typesetting, Romford, Essex
Printed and bound in Great Britain by Biddles Ltd, Guildford, Surrey

Contents

Notes

Abbreviations used in the recipes are as follows:

oz. — ounce	Tbs. — tablespoon
lb. — pound	tsp. — teaspoon
pt. — pint	

Temperature equivalents for electricity or the kitchen range, and gas, are as follows:

250°F — Mark 1	375°F — Mark 6
275°F — Mark 2	400°F — Mark 7
300°F — Mark 3	425°F — Mark 8
325°F — Mark 4	450°F — Mark 9
350°F — Mark 5	

Introduction

We have a friend who is a schoolteacher. Last spring she was staying with us, and whilst admiring a brood of new-born chicks she happened to mention a classroom experience of the previous term. The class had been discussing eggs. Upon being asked where these foods came from, one of her pupils had replied that he thought they came from an egg carton. Pressed, this boy could give no further reply other than that the carton came from 'back o' the shop' somewhere.

That was all. It wasn't very funny, really. But it does symbolize a profoundly disturbing process that is taking place in Western society now. Our traditional environment is becoming remote to us.

For it isn't only egg cartons. Our ways of packaging the environment are many—from nature television programmes, wallets of holiday snaps and guided bus tours (the latter even commonly referred to as 'packaged') right on down to so-called 'natural' cosmetics and so on. Thus with our labels and wrappings, and with technology our shield and sword, do we strive to assert our dominance over nature and possess it completely.

What does this mean in terms of the foods we eat? It means that we can buzz our containers all round the world or put them into cold storage so that we can enjoy out-of-season foodstuffs and the produce of a global environment. By parcelling our animals, our fields and our energy resources into highly intensive production units it means that we can further tailor the product to suit demand, so that nationally we can enjoy certain foods such as hothouse fruits and vegetables and animal produce to excess, at least while there is still a plentiful supply of raw materials. It means that with the help of technology and the study of genetics we are learning to tailor the product in other ways too, such as colour, blandness of taste and smoothness of texture, uniformity of shape and size, and so on. And finally it means that we can seal ourselves off from the actual soil of the fields, from the blood of the animal and the sweat of labour, from our collective memories of poverty and the grind of subsistence living. Altogether it means an inflated sense of wealth and well-being for most of us. Nature provides—as and when we will.

There is, inevitably, a price to be paid. Materially, that price is waste. As an explicit example, there is the waste of our energy and raw material resources and of the world's cereal reserves. Many nutritionalists nowadays freely admit that we could drastically reduce our national intake of meat, eggs and dairy produce. We don't, though an estimated 80%* or more of our total cereal production in this country is utilized for animal feeding stuffs—and this despite the fact that milk wastes 75% of the calories and proteins needed to produce it while eggs waste 78%, poultry 85%, pork 88% and beef 94%. (That is, in addition to quantities of grass and hay it takes up to 7 or 8 pounds of grain to produce one pound of beef!) Indeed, it is arguably a consequence of our insistence on a surfeit of animal produce that we had to import over £600 million worth of cereals in 1975—this being in addition to the £1200 million worth of animal produce and £100 million worth of animal feeding stuffs we also imported in that year. On this scale, of course, transportation itself involves a further massive wastage, that of energy resources. Finally, to all this must be added the expenditure of raw materials on such things as cold storage and food processing plants, fertilizers and insecticides, heated greenhouses and, last but not least, the countless tons of throwaway packaging materials with which we dress up all our foods.

But even expressed explicitly in percentages and statistics, the dimensions of our waste are probably not very meaningful to most of us. Perhaps if we were able to partly translate

*Figures derived from publications by Dr Jean Mayer, Harvard School of Public Health, and Government Statistical Service, Ministry of Agriculture, Fisheries and Food.

them into potential to feed, house, warm and supply the world's needy they might become more so. For instance, as little as one twentieth of the richer nations' meat consumption would, if foregone, release enough grain to feed the populations at present starving in India and Bangladesh. How many sheets of roofing iron could be produced from the metal that goes into our discarded cans, how many windows from the glass that goes into our no-deposit bottles, how many roofing beams from timber that is felled for our superfluous labels and cartons and advertising campaigns, how many calorie hours in a pensioner's bedsit from the oil that is burned to bring us strawberries in midwinter and tomatoes all year round?

Then there is the other side of the coin, the less explicit wastage that we can only begin to guess at. This, of course, is the wastage of the environment itself—the very soil and air and sea that we are supposed to be enjoying, and preserving for the enjoyment of our children. At one level this means the loss of the poppies from our cornfields, the bulldozing of hedgerows, the destruction of birdlife due to the increasing use of insecticides—all attributable to the intensification of farming practices as they try to keep up with the demands of our growing population for the more land-hungry foods already mentioned. At another level it means a further impetus towards more chances of oil slicks on our beaches, more motorways, more pollution of the air through fumes and noise. So it isn't only our children who will pay if our legacy to them is to be a super-egg in a plastic carton, nor the whole world's children only, even if many of them are to have no egg at all. We will pay also, and in a very material way—for something about the product has already begun to smell.

People have been realizing it, in a general sort of way, for quite a while. The mass-produced, standardized consumer article, so costly to produce in the quantities we are addicted to, is under fire on many fronts. But it isn't only environmental awareness in its material form that has led to the resurgence of interest in cottage industry, communes and community workshops, hand-made craft goods and so on.

It is as if people are wanting also to rip off the plastic film and taste again the real quality and substance of life and the world around them. Where exactly, though, does this leave the ecologically-minded cook, if not stranded in the supermarket with an empty shopping basket?

Obviously there must be an answer, for food is the most basic of all our interactions with the environment. What we need to find are ways in which our day-to-day eating habits can bring us into closer contact and greater harmony with it, for the benefit not only of the environment and mankind as a whole, but of ourselves as well. If this means eating less foods that are packaged and processed, unseasonal, global and animal in origin, of what foods does it mean we should eat more? Simply, the answer is that we should eat more foods that are fresh, seasonal, local—and wholesome.

We know a lot of people would want immediately to take us to task over the comparison implied by the last of these categories. Nevertheless we believe it is a valid one and we certainly are not mere faddists. Because of the waste involved, a diet which is basically oriented towards animal products is not a *whole*some diet. In an agriculture such as ours with its high proportion of arable lands, animal foods represent the fat of the land in every sense. We are wasting the environment to produce cream to make the cat smile—a Cheshire-cat smile, if we may be pardoned for saying so, for ultimately the environment cannot waste very much faster than the people dependent upon it.

So which foods are most wholesome? The answer is not hard to find. The foods are those which the country can most happily and bountifully grow—cereals, vegetables, fruits and just a few animal products, particularly from those animals fed on recycled scraps or grazed on non-arable lands with little supplementary feeding of cereals.

The rest then falls into place, for the terms 'fresh', 'local', and 'seasonal' need little explaining in relation to food, and already there is a growing interest in this type of produce. Many readers will be acquainted with the joys of shopping for the freshest vegetables in the early-morning markets, or buying a homebaked cake from a charity stall. There is a new awareness of the importance of providing a local food-source, if it is only a pocket-handkerchief-sized garden or even a window box with a patch of mustard and cress. Seed sales are rocketing, admittedly in part for economic reasons—but our economic plight is not unconnected with the deepening environmental crisis. There is an awakening interest, too, in our wild foods, and so-called health or organic foods have been growing in popularity. The threads are all there in fact; all that is required is to gather them together in a single, unified way. That is what we have tried to do in this book.

For us, personally, the threads began to gather half a decade ago, when we ceased our long travellings from North America and Australia, through all of Europe and a good bit of Asia and the Middle East, and settled on a small croft holding in the Hebrides to do what we felt to be our thing. With us we brought the global environments we had touched upon, not as expensively preserved and transported foods but as recipes we had carried with us in our hearts and minds and notebooks. By adapting those that seemed suitable to our ingredients we began to find what was for us a true balance between past and present, between the world outside and our own fourteen acres of grass and heather, scrub and shore.

At the same time we developed an interest in home wine-making and in brewing teas from local wild herbs or those we had cultivated ourselves. We discovered wild fruits and mushrooms and the produce of the shore. We dug a vegetable garden and we began to keep chickens and to graze a couple of goats on the tough, heathery moors, and what we could not produce ourselves we bought as locally as we could. We began also to experiment with cooking British grains instead of rice, remembering how we had seen the Turks serve wheat, and dredging the local folk histories for recipes for oats. We began to put our recipes down—and at length we began to share them.

Of course, we also put this book together in the knowledge that we are especially fortunate with food-sources in our surroundings. Urban dwellers have to rely heavily on the shops for their foods, whatever their preference. The amount one can produce in a city will always be limited by the size of the garden or, if one is lucky enough to have it, the allotment provided by the local authority. But it is important to remember that the garden grows beyond the urban boundaries, too. Out of the city or township environs foods can be found as fresh and seasonal as you want them—local farm produce in the spring, summer berries and wild herbs, nuts and mushrooms in the autumn, winter shellfish and sea vegetables, to name but a few. So let's taste the environment, instead of eyeing it through the prophylactic barrier of a car window. Then, as our foods become less packaged so do our trips to the countryside—and our attitudes towards it.

It all adds up. We are not advocating a complete return to a hand-to-mouth type of existence, or denying that technology has its better aspects; all we are pleading really is for people to take a greater hand in the preparation of their meals, as it were, from the roots up. For environmental consciousness does begin with the foods we eat, for positive as well as negative reasons. Fresh, local, seasonal and wholesome foods and a fresh, whole-minded, balanced approach to the world we live in do go together—and who can deny that a free-range egg tastes better than a battery-produced one?

And who knows, too, where it may all lead? (For us, as we grew more and more of our own food and became more and more involved with the animals which provided our milk, cheese and eggs, our diet became more and more grain-based until now, although we still eat some fish, we are vegetarians. Fine — if we eat less beef, perhaps we'll have to make better shoes!). As we cease to raid the environmental larder perhaps our other raids upon nature will become less exhausting and we'll find new ways of evaluating ourselves, ways that do not depend upon the per capita consumption of goods. And as we cease to evaluate waste with wealth, as our demands for the mass-produced, instant-happiness, packaged product ease perhaps we'll manage to emancipate ourselves a little from the servitude to the machine technology which thus rewards us. Perhaps, as some followers of more esoteric diets claim, the foods that we eat might even become reflected in our thoughts and feelings by some subtle inner process, leading directly to greater personal happiness and individual balance and harmony.

Perhaps. But this is really getting far beyond the scope of this volume. All we want to do from now on is sit at your table while you get on with the meal. We appreciate how it is to be guests; after all, we ought to, for we both were born quite a few thousand miles away.

IN PASSING . . .

While assembling the recipes for this book we realized just how efficient our kitchen range is. Not only will it burn coal, coke, smokeless fuel, beach wood, peat, old plastic bottles and other combustible rubbish, but it gives us a constant supply of hot water and, most important in connection with this book, a constant cooking and warming surface plus an ever-hot oven, virtually twenty-four hours a day and without worrying about gas or electricity bills.

The range heats our very large kitchen (and we must say there is something eminently cheering about a kettle gently steaming, always ready to make that pot of tea), and heats a drying cupboard adjacent to it in which we dry mushrooms and berries or sprout seeds. It keeps the kitchen ceiling at just the right temperature so that in late summer we can hang herbs, bunches of onions and garlic for drying, from the thick beams, and provides a very low oven ideal for drying out the processed wheat which forms such an important part of our diet. And all this for only keeping one firebox gently and steadily lit!

So, if you have the space in your kitchen, a range is well worth whatever little trouble you may feel it would be to tend it—for the winter and autumn months anyway. For us, our kitchen range is the hub of our home, for around it there is so much happy and warming activity.

Chapter One
The Soil

CEREALS

'Who will help me plant this grain of wheat?' asked the little red hen.
'Not I,' said the duck.
'Not I,' said the dog.
'Not I,' said the cat.
'Then I'll plant it myself,' said the little red hen.
And so she did.

Traditional English Fairy Tale

Not all of us live as close to the soil as little red hen. Not many of us can in this present age. We have been largely displaced from the soil by machines, and cannot really be blamed for not helping if we do not have anything to do with our bread before it arrives on the bakery shelf. The nearest thing for most of us could be a brief stop beside a field of ripening wheat on some weekend trip out of town. Then, for a few moments, we might even touch upon a sort of collective nostalgia for the past. How good, then, to pluck and winnow a small handful and let the grains trickle slowly through our fingers! How complete they feel to the touch. How whole. How self-contained. . .

And so they are. In fact, cereals generally can be considered to be the most complete of all our foods. In her wisdom, little red hen knew that that seed contained the germ of her daily bread. But in a wider sense seeds collectively can be thought of as containing the germ of almost all that is life-sustaining, not only for plants and hens but for ourselves as well. This applies equally to vegetarians and non-vegetarians alike, for all our domestic animals are dependent ultimately on the plant life generated by seeds. Thus they are the primary living intermediaries between man and his environment. Seeds are dependent directly upon the cycle of the seasons. Their own patterns of regeneration bring them back to the soil every year. For the key to a better relationship with the environment, then, it is surely towards seeds that we should look--and in particular towards cereals, our most important edible seeds.

The wholesomeness of cereals is reflected in their nutritional values (see Protein Chart, p.11). They store readily all year round and make the most efficient use of the land. So in this first chapter, where we shall endeavour to list all the domesticated and wild foods that the soil produces for us, and their places in the ecologically balanced diet, it seemed most natural in every way to begin with these foods. They are, after all, the most basic of all in our diets.

Commercially, four cereals are grown in this country (though an enterprising farmer might well experiment with others, such as buckwheat). These four are wheat, oats, barley and rye. Together they provide enough variety to satisfy our own personal wants, without our having to have recourse at all to rice or other imported cereals. They can be eaten whole as cooked grains or in some slightly processed or pre-cooked form, or ground and cooked as flours or meals either individually or in combination. For us they provide, in fact, the basis for most main-course dishes. This is sound nutritional as well as sound ecological practice, as the table on the following page makes clear.

Although it can be seen that whole cereals are inferior to animal products in proteins, they do make up for this by being superior to the potatoes which we eat in such large quantities nationally to balance our meat intake. Indeed, a diet comprised largely of cereals supplemented by a variety of vegetables and some nuts or beans or just a very small proportion of animals products (to provide the few proteins lacking in cereals) is of itself a balanced diet. So important, then, are our cereals, that it is necessary to give each of the four individual treatment in this chapter.

PROTEIN CHART

All figures quoted as grams per hundred grams (percentage by weight) of the fresh product except in the case of legumes. Figures for these are based on the form the produce is generally sold in, i.e., dried.

Figures for most products depend on condition of product (fat content of meat, etc.) as well as such factors as time and place of growing, and are therefore often variable and are here given as approximate.

Product	Protein Content
Lean pork	29
Steak	25
Chicken	23
Lamb (rib chop)	20
Cheddar cheese	25
Cod	18
Eggs	12
Wheat (hard red)	13
Oats (dehusked)	13
Rye	11.5
Barley	9.5
Rice (polished)	6.5
Soybeans	34
Lentils	26
Peanuts	28
Kidney beans	24
Chickpeas	22
Broad beans	26
Tic beans (field beans)	25
English walnuts	15
Potatoes	2
Most green veg. (except legumes)	3—4

In appraising various dishes for their protein content, however, it should be borne in mind that because of the complimentary nature of amino acids in cereals and legumes the total usable protein content of a mixed cereal-legume dish is up to thirty per cent greater than the sum of its usable parts (the body wastes a certain amount of the protein content of all foods). Cereals and dairy products have a similar though lesser protein complimentary role, as do legumes and dairy products.

Thus it can be seen that a mixed cereal-legume dish, or a cereal-based dish served with some dairy produce and with or without legumes, compares very favourably with the meat-potato combination which is our traditional national mainstay! Even a cereal dish served with vegetables and a very small quantity of meat compares well with a larger quantity of meat eaten with potatoes.

Wheat

Almost everyone eats wheat flour daily in one form or another. Of all cereals wheat has the second highest protein content and most people know the nutritional importance of eating wholewheat flour products whenever possible; fewer, however, know that you can use the whole grains themselves as a basis for a meal. This is possible simply by soaking overnight then boiling the grains like rice in salted water for about half an hour, before draining and serving with the other ingredients.

However, boiled whole wheat, while very palatable, requires a little more chewing than our relatively unexercised jaw muscles are used to. One or two recipes for wheat and rye cooked in this way are nevertheless included, but most of our recipes for these grains call for a pre-cooked form which we find more easily chewed and very versatile. We discovered the recipe ourselves by experiment, after many unsuccessful attempts to prise the secret of bulghur making from uncommunicative Turks. In fact, it may well be nearly the same thing as bulghur. We simply call it pre-cooked wheat and use it as a basis for our main meal about twice a week or so. It has, incidentally, a very distinctive nutty flavour which has never failed to please even our most suspicious and conservative of guests.

BASIC PRE-COOKED WHEAT RECIPE

Whole, unrefined wheat grains
Water

Wash and strain enough wheat grains to fill a one-gallon bucket or large pot about half to two-thirds full. (Less can be prepared at once if required; see below.) Fill container with water to the top, cover, and leave grains to soak in a cool place for three days. After soaking the grains should have swollen by a third of their original volume and taken up enough water to have made them quite soft. A little fermentation may have begun to take place, depending on the temperature of storage, but this is in no way harmful to the nutritional or taste value of the eventual product.

Wash and strain the soaked grains again, drain and spread on shallow baking trays so that each is covered to a depth of no more than half an inch. (Five or six trays of average size, i.e., enough to occupy all the grids in the oven, should take the indicated quantity of grain.) Place trays in oven and bake slowly at the lowest mark possible. This is best done very slowly over a number of hours or preferably overnight. For this purpose an old-fashioned coal- or wood-burning range with a firebox full of dying coals is ideal, but a gas or electric oven, turned down, will do.

When ready the grains should be hard, slightly wrinkled and a golden to straw brown colour on the outside. Inside, the grains should be lighter. They can now be cracked, either in an old fashioned coffee grinder adjusted to its coarsest setting or in a grain mill, a tool which can be purchased from hardware merchants and well worth the initial small investment, especially if you like grinding some of your own flour as well. If neither grinder or mill is available, you could crack enough in a strong piece of canvas, using a hammer, to give an idea of the taste. But whatever method is used, the pieces should be variable, with some smaller pieces and some to half a grain in size.

The wheat can now be stored indefinitely, and will provide 4-6 people with about eight meals. Though it sounds like a lot of trouble, the whole process soon becomes a matter of routine, requiring only a few minutes' attention at each stage. Still, it is worthwhile saving on fuel and time to do as much as possible at once. For individual meals the cracked and pre-cooked grain is generally boiled as follows:

2 cups pre-cooked wheat
4 cups water
Salt

Bring the salted water to the boil and then add pre-cooked wheat. Simmer for twenty-five minutes and then remove from flame and let steam for a few more minutes with the lid removed from the pot.

The wheat can now be served with a side-dish or sauce, or it can be turned into a casserole or stew. It can be fried in pancakes or rissoles or baked, in combination with other ingredients, as a kind of 'wheatloaf' (suggestive in appearance, texture and even in taste of meatloaf). It can be used as a basis for soups and stuffings or it can be boiled with more than the usual amount of water and served as a breakfast cereal. Altogether it is one of the most versatile foods we have ever come across, and there seems to be little loss of nutritional value in the redistribution of proteins and hydrolysis of starches that apparently takes place. Perhaps it is these changes, characteristic of the malting process used in brewing, etc., that give the grain its full, nutty taste. This recipe serves 4-6.

CRACKED OR ROASTED WHEAT

This is another, and shorter, method of breaking down the stickiness of wheat and preparing it for the table. The taste is distinctive and somewhat different from the pre-cooked grain, but although good we find it not quite so versatile as the other and use it most often at short notice, when it is of course more convenient.

2 cups wheat grains
Salt to taste

Wash and drain the wheat grains. Place the grains in a shallow tray in a slow oven, or pan-roast with a little salt over a medium heat, stirring constantly. The grains are ready when all the water has evaporated. If pan-roasted (the shortest method of all) this will be accompanied by cracking and jumping, as in popping corn.

Remove pan or tray, coarse-grind the grains in a mill and simmer gently for twenty-five minutes, if necessary in water further salted to taste. The cooked grains can be served with a sauce or side-dish. Serves 4-6.

OTHER WHEAT PRODUCTS

As well as in a whole form, wheat can be bought as flaked or rolled grains like rolled oats. Unlike cooked rolled oats however, cooked flaked wheat grains are not so mushy, especially if you buy them toasted, and they can be very good in casseroles and soups as well as in crunchy pie crusts, biscuits, etc. For individual recipes using wheat flakes or any other wheat products, consult the index.

Whole wheat grains and wheat products, including flaked grains and wholewheat flours, can be purchased from most health food shops, grain stores and macrobiotic and wholefood stores—the latter can increasingly be found in most larger cities and with prices that compete favourably with the larger chain stores. For the cheapest grains of all, however, go to the corn and agricultural merchants who supply farmers, where the price per half-hundredweight can be as little as one-sixth that of imported long-grain rice, for example. If buying from these sources, though, it is important to check that you are getting ripe, clean and full-bodied grain from the previous season's crop, and that it has not been adulterated with fish oil.

Rye

Rye has so many characteristics in common with wheat that it is scarcely necessary to mention it under a separate heading. It can be dry-roasted, boiled after soaking or after pre-cooking, or purchased ground as a flour. Rye has an unusual spicy taste, however, and it is good to keep a jar on hand for variety whichever way you feel like preparing it. Rye flour, too, has something special that makes it very good in breads, chappatis and pancakes.

However, it is often difficult to obtain rye. Though rye flour is generally on sale in health food and macrobiotic shops, whole rye grain is less easy to find. It is best to order this in bulk from an organic farm or specialist grain store.

Oats

Oats have one of the highest protein contents of all cereals. When a Scot claims that it is his morning bowl of porridge that puts the brawn on his back he might be closer to the truth than we suspect, for oatmeal porridge taken with milk is almost a whole food in itself. If he ate nothing other than a few cabbages, carrots and some salad greens, a man could probably live out his life in as much health as most of us attain.

There's no need to confine our oats to the porridge pot, however, for in another form they can provide us with a staple food quite as useful and easy to prepare as rice. In this form they are called groats.

Groats are simply the whole kernel of the oat grain with the outer husk removed. Though slightly smaller, they have something of the appearance of unpolished long-grain rice. Boiled as an alternative to rice they are, if very slightly chewier, quite delicious—and quite uncharacteristic of anything you've ever tasted, including porridge.

BASIC BOILED GROATS

2 cups groats
6 cups water
Good pinch of salt

Wash the groats well, strain and then simmer slowly in the boiling salted water for 25 minutes, or until the grains are just beginning to split. Drain and rinse several times in a collander under the hot tap or with boiling water from the kettle to remove the starch. If cooked and rinsed well, the groats should be light and not sticky, firm and whole without being chewier than brown rice. The water in which the groats were cooked can be saved as a thickener for soups. Serves 4-6 people.

Other Oat Products

As well as providing us with hot breakfast, oatmeal and rolled oats can be used to advantage in a number of varied recipes.

Both are good in pancakes, breads, biscuits and other baked goods, while rolled oats are especially great for crunchy pie crusts. Oatmeal and rolled oats are, of course, available in most supermarkets but for groats you'll have to try the health food shops, specialist grain stores and wholefood stores.

Barley

Barley is lower in protein and higher in carbohydrates than our other grains. It is also lighter and blander. We use the whole grain mostly in soups and casseroles, though the cereal can be cooked and served in the same way as groats, from which it makes a nice change from time to time. The cooked grain finds a particular place on our table served cold in summer salads, where its lightness becomes an advantage.

Like oats and wheat, barley can also be bought as flaked grains. Barley flakes are good for adding crunchiness to biscuits, pie crusts and other baked goods. They are also good in soups because they thicken readily without dissolving to a complete paste. Barley flour can be used instead of oatmeal in such things as pancakes too. But, rather than give proportions here, just experiment yourself with adding different flours or flaked grains to your ordinary recipes in your own proportions. It's amazing what a difference this can make.

For barley and barley products you'll have to go to the usual sources, as explained above. Pearl barley for soups is, of course, more widely available.

VEGETABLES

If cereals provide us with the basis for most of our main-course dishes, it is to the vegetable kingdom that we look for the most important variations in flavour and texture. Vegetables in addition, are the most important ingredients of our soups. In fact, they add variety as well as important nutritional elements to any meal in which they are served and in the ecologically balanced, meat-reduced diet, a plentiful supply of fresh vegetables is essential. Happily, these foods, because of the ease of their cultivation and their direct relationships with the soil and seasons, are able to provide many of us with a bridge to the environment which corresponds in importance to the place they should occupy in our diets.

Almost everyone, in fact, should be able to grow a few pot-herbs or a patch of greens somewhere close to hand. When you do buy vegetables, choose those which are fresh, seasonal and as local as you can find them; it's the next best thing to growing your own. On the following page is a list of vegetables which can be grown out of doors or in unheated greenhouses in this country, together with the natural seasons of availability.

From this list it can be seen that the soil is quite capable of providing us with a varied supply of vegetables all year round, without our ever having to have recourse to wasteful cultivation and preservation techniques. In fact, some root vegetables (e.g., carrots, parsnips, winter radishes) can themselves be considered to be available more or less at any time because they stand for long periods in the soil and can also be stored easily under natural conditions. Cultivated mushrooms are likewise considered because they can be grown throughout the year in boxes of fermenting compost. Finally, special mention must be made of haricot and soya beans which, as well as being delicious fresh in season, can also be readily dried, providing high protein foods for use throughout the year, and as such are of great potential importance to our diets.

But a bean which is just recently becoming available again, is the little tic bean, relative of the broad bean. There has only been a limited success growing the high-protein soya bean in the south of England, but the little tic bean *can* be grown anywhere in Britain, gives a good yield, and when dried is high in protein—in excess of twenty per cent.

We tried some this past summer and were very happy with the results--from two small rows we gathered and dried enough beans to plant a large plot next year, a plot which should yield us enough for the year's use. We also ate some of the beans and found them very delicious indeed.

VEGETABLES WHICH CAN BE GROWN OUT-OF-DOORS OR IN UNHEATED GREENHOUSES

Name	Months of Availability*	Name	Months of Availability*
American cress	Aug.-May	Dandelion	Dec.-May
Artichoke, globe	June-Aug.	Endive	Nov.-Feb.
Artichoke, Jerusalem	Nov.-Jan.	Kale, curly	Oct.-Mar.
Asparagus	Aug.-Sept.	Kale, sea beet or Swiss chard	July-Sept.
Aubergine	Aug.-Sept.	Kohl Rabi	June-Sept.
Beans:		Leek	Sept.-Jan.
Broad	June-Sept.	Lettuce	June-Sept.
Dwarf, runner	July-Aug.	Marrow	Aug.-Sept.
French	Aug.	Onion	July onwards
Haricot	Aug.-Sept.	Onion, spring	Mar.-May
Soya	Aug.-Sept.	Parsley	July-Nov.
Tic	Sept.-Oct.	Parsley, Hamburg	Sept. onwards
Beetroot	July onwards	Parsnip	July onwards
Broccoli	Nov.-May	Pea	July-Aug.
Brussels sprouts	Sept.-March	Potato	July onwards
Cabbage	Oct.-June	Pumpkin	Aug.-Sept.
Cabbage, Chinese	Aug.-Oct.	Radish, red	June-Sept.
Capsicum	Aug.-Sept.	Radish, Winter	
Carrot	July onwards	Black	Nov.-April
Cauliflower	Sept.-Dec.	Red	Nov.-April
Celeriac	Oct.-Feb.	Salsify	Nov.-April
Celery	Sept.-Nov.	Scorzonera	Sept.-April
Chicory	Nov.-May	Tomato	July-Sept.
Corn, sweet	Aug.-Sept.	Turnip	July onwards
Cucumber	July-Sept.	Mushrooms (edible fungi)	All year round
Courgette	Aug.-Sept.		

*Months are approximate generalisations of course: much depends on local conditions. For example, up here on Skye we are able to have fresh parsley well into the winter, sometimes right up until the early spring. (Gardeners in the southern hemisphere can convert this table to their own climate simply by adding six months to the months above. Thus August becomes February, November becomes May, and so on.)

Apparently there are others following suit, for a friend of mine recently heard the beans' virtues extolled on a North of Scotland farm programme, the narrator recommending that farmers grow them as a viable crop. Another friend in Bristol tells me that you can buy tic beans out of big burlap sacks in some of the local stores.* So, if they're not available in your area yet, and you can't grow them (seeds are available from Thompson & Morgan, Seedsmen), then they should be available soon.

Providing Your Own

Unfortunately, a vegetable's natural season of availability as listed in the chart does not necessarily mean its season of availability in the nearby supermarket or even at the local greengrocer's. Thus some, such as tomatoes, may be on the shelves very much out of season while others, such as scorzonera, could as well refer to hamlets in Siberia for all that we are familiar with them. This is because commercial market gardeners are hampered by what they consider to be the optimum use of their resources and the general level of demand—as well, of course, as the size of the profits they want to make. So it is even more important to grow your own vegetables if at all possible.

If you're limited to a pocket-handkerchief-sized piece of land, concentrate on those types which are best for variety but difficult to obtain. Of these we would especially recommend asparagus, globe artichokes (which make a beautiful addition to a flower garden),† late broccoli, salad spinach, Chinese cabbage, endives, chicory, Jerusalem artichokes, winter radishes, celeriac, Hamburg parsley, salsify and scorzonera. The last six mentioned are root vegetables, perfect for subtle soups and vegetable dishes in the autumn and winter when our instincts withdraw to our sheltering abodes, to 'go to earth' ourselves as it were. Then in spring,

*In January 1976 tic beans were available in Bristol at £9.45 per cwt.

†There are many advantages to mixing fruit, vegetables, and flowers in your garden, or 'companion planting' as it is known. See Bibliography for further reading.

when other vegetables are short, we can begin a new cycle with sprouting plants like broccoli, asparagus and forcing chicory. In summer we can draw upon the rich profusion and variety the season offers by adding our own salad spinach, Chinese cabbage or globe artichokes to the produce commonly available in the shops. With a little ingenuity and imagination so much can be done with a small garden—globe artichokes, as mentioned above, and asparagus look as well in the flower garden as in the vegetable patch behind the house, while Jerusalem artichokes planted along a fence can make a fine screen. But however big or small your garden, do try to avoid using artificial fertilizers, pesticides and weed-killers, wherever possible.

In praising the virtues of the domestic vegetable, however many there may be, we must not forget that there is another tribe in the kingdom worth mentioning in the present context too—the edible wild plants. We have an ample garden and are disinclined towards the sometimes stronger tastes of wild plants, with a few exceptions: especially in March, when there is often little available, we use young stinging nettles and chickweed to augment dwindling garden vegetables. But the keen forager can supply himself with an alternative supply of fresh vegetables in the form of young tender thistle shoots, water lily roots (although unless one is really hungry it seems a shame to kill our beautiful lilies), sorrel, dock, and so forth if he chooses. Beginners are recommended to read Richard Mabey's book (listed in the Bibliography).

Now to those wild vegetables which we do feel deserve a special mention. First amongst these are the best of the common root vegetables—dandelion and burdock. Both can be found in the cultivated form, dandelion at home and burdock in Japan where it is prized as a domestic vegetable. The dried and roasted roots of either make a fine, health-giving substitute for coffee. Burdock can also be a delicious vegetable in its own right, while the young dandelion leaves make a passable salad or cooked green vegetable in spring when other greens are short.

Next comes a group of sea-vegetables: carageen, dulse, lettuce laver and the like. Like burdock, sea-vegetables are prized as foods in Japan but except in times of poverty or war we have made scanty use of them in Britain. This seems a pity, for as well as being highly nutritious—dulse, for example, is about twenty per cent protein—they can be very palatable if cooked and served in the right way. And, after all, like the Japanese, we are an island people.

For the final mention in this section we have saved our favourite of all groups of vegetables, wild or domesticated, in the kingdom—a group which, in fact, can more properly be considered fruits than vegetables, though it is more convenient to consider them under the latter heading. We are talking of wild edible fungi. So much more could be made of our wild mushrooms and toadstools in this country. We'll eat the cultivated mushroom, perhaps even the common field mushrooms, but for some reason the very mention of toadstools is enough to turn people pale, while the idea of actually eating them, as is common on the continent (in France over thirty varieties are sold commercially while in Munich ten times that number are licensed for sale at the famous fungi market) seems positively suicidal. Yet, to get the whole thing in perspective, of the thousand or so different species of large fungi growing in this country, there are less than a dozen which could be described as deadly poisonous, and more than half of these are very uncommon or rare. Against that there are scores of edible varieties, a lot of them better than the cultivated mushroom, a few of them quite exquisite. There are wild fungi on our own table once or twice a week from the middle of August through to the end of October, and we've suffered nary a tummy ache.

Of course there is no reason for not identifying fungi, like other wild vegetables, with the utmost thoroughness and caution. One must always use a field guide and follow its instructions to the letter (see Bibliography) and the beginner would, in addition, be best served by obtaining the services of an experienced friend if at all possible. But once we are sure of our prize, there is no better way to savour an autumn visit to the forest than with a dish of wild fungi, rich and redolent of their aromatic woodland environment. Anyway, in the hopes of being able to share the experience we've included several recipes for fungi dishes in the chapter on autumn (Ch. 4). Each is based on a readily identifiable species with which it is impossible even for the inexperienced gatherer to go wrong.

Preparation of Vegetables

For many dishes the method of cutting vegetables is almost as important as the method of cooking them. They may be chopped, diced, shredded, eaten whole or sliced laterally, diagonally or longitudinally. Most, including mushrooms, may then be boiled, steamed, pressure-cooked, baked, deep fried, sautéd, pickled or eaten raw in salads and sandwiches. But, especially in preparing greens, it is important not to overcook them.

Apart from soups, chutneys or salads, most vegetables are eaten in main-course dishes though a few, such as carrots and pumpkins, can be used in sweets and desserts. For the cook with access to a ready and varied supply there is, in fact, virtually no limit to the different combinations of cereals and vegetables that can be achieved with a little imagination.

MEAT, FISH, EGGS AND DAIRY PRODUCTS

For reasons outlined in the introduction, animal foods are considered to be of minor importance in the ecologically balanced diet. With the exception of very special feast dishes and occasional omelettes or leg of lamb, they should be regarded as secondary.

As can be seen from the figures on p. 2, meat is especially wasteful to produce. It should generally be used very sparingly. Sheep, however, are naturally suited to our rough hill and moorland grazings, so there should be a certain place for mutton and lamb in our diets, especially spring lamb. Beef, on the other hand, should be eaten seldom, though the overall necessity to retain some dairy herds might provide us with a justification for eating a little veal now and then. Pork, bacon and chicken, too, could be eaten sparingly from time to time, as chickens and pigs recycle waste foods for us. Of these foods we would tend more towards chicken, since chickens are more efficient feeders, and on free range will eat almost anything, including slugs and insect pests. Also, free-range chicken is a natural by-product of free-range egg production in contrast, it must be noted, to the produce of battery caged birds which are generally bred for the table or for eggs.

The case for reducing our consumption of fish rests upon a different basis altogether—the over-exploitation of the seas which is generally acknowledged to have taken place in so many fishing grounds throughout the world. Fish are a direct gift to us from nature, and to the ecologically-minded person the need for overall moderation in our diets must be self-evident. One way of achieving this might be to avoid seasonal overkill in the form of canned and frozen fish, a practice which also makes ecological sense for other reasons mentioned in this book.

Moderation is also called for as far as eggs and dairy products are concerned, though there is some justification for eating these foods a little more often than meat. Eggs, milk and milk products are the most economical animal foods to produce as well as being among the most versatile ingredients in our cookery. And who knows how the ecological scales would decide between imported vegetable oils and home produced butter, or between some animal foods, best represented by eggs and dairy products, and the quantities of imported beans which would otherwise be required to provide the necessary protein in the diets of our children?

We certainly don't. Nor is it that important, of course.

Our food doesn't have to be sifted through graph paper or stirred with a slide rule. It must be prepared with zest and joy and in basic communion with the countryside, not in the cold light of a self-effacing analysis of it. This book therefore contains a few recipes for beans (although we hope tic beans will be used and not any of the imported ones) and a few more for dishes using eggs and dairy products, and even one or two for using both. It contains recipes using butter, recipes using oil and recipes that call for butter or oil. The most important thing simply is general moderation—eating what you feel is right and avoiding one or two pitfalls like compensating for a reduced meat diet intake by over-eating eggs and dairy products. For as well as being self-defeating, the latter might well be downright unhealthy. Some authorities claim that eggs in excess are bad for the blood and digestive systems, while milk is a mammary fluid primarily intended for the suckling of young by their parent animals and not for wholly indiscriminate use by humans. We should try to cut down on eggs and dairy products despite other dietary changes, substituting cereals, vegetables and nuts, etc.

Animal foods, when they are purchased, should be subject to the same rules as the rest of our foods. With the exception of cheese, all animal products should be bought in as fresh a condition as they can be found—in the case of fish and some meats this maximises our chances of buying produce that is seasonal, too. We should also persist in asking about the history of foods and try to obtain meat from a local abbatoir, fish from a local port and dairy foods from a local dairy. Small, independent retailers might provide our best chance of doing this. We should insist on free-range eggs, often available from health-food shops, and free-range chickens too. We might have to give up eating eggs altogether from November to January and go to a good butcher for our chicken, but in taste alone the experience would be more than worth it. In fact, we should avoid whenever possible all animal foods which are intensively produced in artificial environments, for our own sakes as well as the animals'. Through the eating of the animal its environment becomes our own. And who wants to become a battery hen?

Providing Your Own

Animal foods do not offer as much scope for home production as vegetables, but there are nevertheless unexplored possibilities open to a lot of us. As pointed out in the Introduction, many suburban backyards could house and exercise three or four scrap-fed chickens in a wired-off corner. And there must be a number of people living around the outskirts of towns who have an empty shed and access to half an acre of waste land that could graze a milch goat or two. Goats are less selective feeders than cows, require little attention and certainly deserve an increasingly prominent place among domestic animals in these troubled times.

Wild animals, on the other hand, afford most of us an ever-decreasing chance of providing something for the table. There can be few real hunters or even poachers left nowadays, and fewer birds and beasts of game left for them to stalk, with the exception of private deer, grouse and pheasants and, of course, our common rabbits and hares. Of the land animals, in fact, rabbits and hares are about the only means of providing anything wild for the pot.

More rewarding than the land for catching something though, might be the nation's rivers and inshore waters from which it is still possible for the keen angler to bring home a modest bag.

Preparation of Meat, Fish, Eggs and Dairy Products

In ecologically balanced cookery we feel that meat should almost always be chopped or diced for use in main-course dishes. It will then go further and at the same time have the happy side effect of complementing cereals and vegetables in a subtle interaction of flavours, instead of dominating the entire course as so often happens in meat-heavy meals. For this reason meat should generally be sautéd with vegetables or used in conjunction with them in soups, stews, casseroles, pies, etc.

Fish, with the possible exception of seafood (shellfish), does not lend itself so easily to the same treatment, unfortunately. More often than not we find it necessary to serve fish whole or in cuts. Even so, we should usually be able to maintain a balance with the rest of the course by serving it with plenty of complementary vegetables or perhaps as a side dish. Remember that a balanced meal reflects a balanced attitude of mind, and that it is upon balanced attitudes that a balanced environment will ultimately depend.

As in almost all cookbooks, eggs and dairy products are to be found as ingredients in a variety of dishes in the following pages, though perhaps not in such a wide variety as they are found in some collections of recipes. Still, we use eggs in baking, soups, pancakes, as well as in one or two special-occasion dishes like our version of Egg Foo Yung. Cheese, too, finds a place for itself in several main-course dishes, especially baked as a topping for casseroles or in pies. Cream is used occasionally in sauces and dips. The dairy product we personally use most extensively, however, is yoghurt, which is easy to make at home, economical (there being no wastage in the form of whey—although whey can be used in soups and in baking, especially for bread) and a natural accompaniment to many vegetable and some meat dishes. The children love it best, however, served as the Turks do in their sweet shops, with a snow-white mound of sifted icing sugar on top.

FRUITS AND NUTS

Fruits and nuts provide us with another and quite dissimilar range of secondary foods for use in our cookery. Personally we would rank them almost with animal foods in importance. They find a different place for themselves of course, being more connected, generally, with desserts than with main-course dishes. But this does not detract from their role in cookery; in fact, it might even be said to enhance it. Thus fruits in a dessert, for example, may complement cheese in a main-course dish in a way which might not be possible if they were served together. Just as each course needs to be harmonised and balanced, so does the overall meal, and for this reason nuts and fruits will often suggest themselves for one or other of the courses when we are planning a menu.

Because that course is most often dessert it does not follow that we have to so confine them. Just as eggs and dairy products can be used in cakes, puddings, etc., so can nuts and even fruits be used in main-course cookery. We use nuts in a number of different ways—they can be great, for example, in salads. Using more nuts as we use less meat makes ecological sense too, for walnuts, hazelnuts, chestnuts and bitter almonds can all be grown in this country. The trees can serve a decorative function as well as a utilitarian one and all could be grown much more extensively, without encroaching much on existing farm lands, in parks, copses, forests, reserves and even waste places. Or they could be grown where trees are needed for shelter and protection, or even for their timber. Hazel trees already grow wild along cliffs and banks and country lanes, and make excellent hedges. Chestnuts and walnuts would become much more plentiful if only forestry groups would utilize the trees, which produce excellent hardwoods and beautiful, lasting furniture, instead of some of the quick-profit softwoods which are being planted almost to the exclusion of other trees at present. As a high protein, easy-to-store food, nuts in fact seem able to compete favourably with meat on almost every count. Even in small quantities they are thus altogether excellent for adding taste and texture to a wide range of dishes, both sweet and savoury.

Fruits, likewise, can be very good in a variety of dishes though they do suffer the disadvantage in our temperate climate, of being very seasonal foods that do not store easily under natural conditions. Thus one must eat some imported fruits or face the prospect of eating virtually no fruits, except stored apples, from the middle of winter to the beginning of the following summer when the first berries are coming along. We feel that we can manage to satisfy our requirements and still maintain a balance with the soil and the seasons by eating lots of fresh fruits in salads and fruity desserts during the summer and autumn, then switching through late winter and spring when apples are scarce, to dried fruits. Sun-dried raisins, sultanas, dates, apricots, prunes, currants, apples and pears seem to find a natural place for themselves in our spicy winter dishes and all can be produced and transported here at a relatively low ecological cost. Not that we feel too bad if we do happen to eat a fresh orange from time to time, or a real treat like a pineapple or, for that matter, a bag of Brazil nuts or pistachios. For, like spices (see p. 31), these are not the foods that are breaking the camel's back. If we practice moderation, so as to savour each just as we might a journey to its country of origin, then we cannot really go far wrong.

Providing Your Own

Anyone with a reasonably-sized kitchen garden can find room for a few fruiting plants. Planting a nut tree, while highly desirable, is generally planting for posterity. The same can be said for pear trees. But with a little knowledge, raspberry, gooseberry and blackcurrant bushes can be made to give quick returns. Even an apple tree will fruit within several years of planting and in bush form a pair will not take up much room. Whether or not you grow your own, however, you may wish in times of glut to preserve fruits for winter use. Drying is an admirable way and a possible means of providing your own dried fruits. Jam-making, another way of preserving fruits, helps reduce waste by making use of discarded jars from commercial brands of jam.

Picking wild berries and nuts in the summer and autumn months can be a delightful pastime, too. Blackberries, raspberries, bilberries and hazelnuts are the most common booty but sloes, elder and rowan berries and rosehips are widespread also, and make excellent jams and jellies. On top of this there are numbers of less common fruits and berries which can amply reward a day's foraging with a little luck. Again, a field guide is recommended for the beginner.

Preparation of Fruits and Nuts

Nuts for use in main-course dishes and desserts can be chopped, ground into meal or added whole and halved. They are especially good with hot or very spicy foods, or those containing sweet ingredients. For this reason fruits often go along well with nuts, whatever the dish. But we find a special place for fruits in chutneys too, and they are also invaluable in home wine-making. See the sections on pickles and chutneys in each chapter, and Home Winemaking, pp. 220-25.

HERBS, SPICES, SEEDS AND SEASONINGS

Under this rather broad heading we lump all the final ingredients of cookery, the subtle tints and tones if you like, that give a dish its finish and distinction. Because we use relatively very little of these simple-to-store foods it does not seem necessary to argue against importing a few from warmer countries of the world. Spices were one of the first-ever goods to be traded among nations; we hope that they will be one of the last.

Personally, we feel free to draw on a range of condiments from all over the world. For it is precisely these foods which bring with them the essence of their countries of origin, so that through the dash and flavour imparted to our cookery they convey to us, when used, the sense of an environment greater than our own. They bring the whole world around us into perspective, and round everything off just perfectly.

As a footnote it must be said though, that in doing so we do confine ourselves to natural foods, since these by definition represent a more balanced interaction with the environment than artificial chemical seasonings like monosodium glutamate. Thus we find most of our needs in the local health food store, making the most of foods such as tahini (a ground sesame product), soya sauce and miso, a fermented product of soya beans and a delicious flavouring for soups and gravies.

Providing Your Own

Whatever may be said of the rest of the foods under this heading, herbs most definitely are not confined to tropical countries. The ecologically-minded cook with access even to a modest-sized piece of land or even just a window box is therefore urged to experiment with a herb garden. Most herbs are expensively and wastefully packaged in small containers but a garden can supply a household, from as little as a couple of square yards, with almost all the herbs it will need throughout the year. And those you have grown and dried yourself taste so much more pungent! Sage, thyme, sweet basil, marjoram, rosemary, coriander, dill, fennel, balm, parsley, garlic and chives are among the most common types that can be grown in this country. And then there is also the lovely bay tree, which is not impartial to shade. With a little practice in identification, there are also the field and woodland herbs, such as juniper, cowberry leaves, elder flowers, peppermint and heathers which can be added to the list, enabling us to sample what is most aromatic in our wild as well as domesticated environment.

Preparation of Herbs, Spices, Seeds and Seasonings

This category covers such a wide range of foods that there is no point in making any special notes about them, outside individual recipes, with two exceptions.

The first concerns the making of wines from wild ingredients such as elder and dandelion flowers, which are best considered as herbs. Though serious wine-making is beyond the scope of this book, several recipes are given. If you've never made wine before, you may want to try one, for winemaking can be fascinating and very rewarding. There's nothing better at Christmas, for example, than inviting your guests to dine over a bottle of your own special wine, the secret of its rarity lying in its locality.

Secondly and finally, there is a small section in the Summer chapter (Ch. 3) of this book devoted to the making of herbal teas. Teas can be made from many cultivated and wild herbs, and the combinations of those that can be used are almost infinite in number. For those who like their tea mild, straight and delicately flavoured a switch to herbal beverages can be a delightful experience in sensual gratification. For herbs, like the rest of the produce in the garden, have a habit of growing on you.

Chapter Two
Spring

SOUPS

Some of the best soups just happen—being made from left-overs laced with miso—and can't be repeated. Others follow a few basic rules, particularly paying attention to the kind of liquid used. It is always a good idea to save water from boiling vegetables, especially beans. Then, of course, there is potato water—either the water in which the potatoes were boiled or, if you peel your potatoes, save the peels and boil these, preferably with a bay leaf or a pinch of mint; strain out the skins and use this water when stock is called for in any recipes.

NETTLE SOUP

Pick nettles when young, or just use the tops of older plants, wash well and chop. And remember, of course, to wear gloves!

1 lb. (approx.) nettles, chopped
1 large onion, sliced
2 large potatoes, washed, cubed
1 Tbs. butter, marge, or enough oil to cover bottom of pan
2 pts. whey or
1 pt. milk (sour if possible) and
1 pt. water (or stock)
1 clove garlic, crushed
Salt, black pepper

Heat oil, or melt butter or marge, in large pot. Cook onion until transparent, then add chopped nettles, potatoes, salt and pepper. Cover tightly and cook for about fifteen to twenty minutes, or until the potato is soft. If the vegetables start to stick, add enough water to keep them from sticking. When all is cooked, add whey, or water and milk and the crushed garlic clove. Heat to simmering, and serve with thick pieces of toast with grated cheese floating in each bowl.

SORREL SOUP

3 good handfuls of sorrel leaves
1 doz. spring onions
2 pts. stock (preferably potato peel water cooked with a pinch of mint)
1 Tbs. cornflour
1 Tbs. butter
Chopped parsley
Salt, black pepper
A little grated nutmeg

Wash and roughly chop the sorrel, finely chop the spring onions, and put both to sauté in the butter. When the sorrel has turned bright green add the stock, saving a few tablespoons to mix with the cornflour. Let simmer for about five minutes, while mixing the cornflour into a paste with the stock. Add this to the soup and cook until thickened. Season to taste with the salt, pepper and the grated nutmeg, and before serving sprinkle finely-chopped parsley on top.

WATERCRESS AND BARLEY SOUP

1 large bunch watercress
1 large onion, sliced, or 6-12 spring onions, chopped
1 cup (or more if desired) cooked barley, washed and drained
2 Tbs. butter
2 pts. stock
1 or 2 cloves garlic, crushed
Soya sauce to taste
Salt, black pepper

Melt butter in heavy saucepan and cook onions until transparent. Add barley to brown slightly, then add watercress and stock. Bring to simmering point, adding salt, pepper, soya sauce and finally the garlic. When heated nicely, garnish with chopped, hard-boiled egg.

EGG DROP SOUP

Spring is a natural time for culling flocks if you keep chickens; then you have the young, unwanted cockerels from the new season's brood, the old cocks who've done their thing and then brought the hens into lay for another season, and the old hens who are not quite up to scratch for another year's laying, to be gotten rid of. The following is a good recipe for an old cock or chicken, suitable for boiling but not broiling or frying.

2 pts. chicken broth
1 cup minced chicken
12-18 spring onions, chopped
3 eggs, beaten
2 Tbs. cornflour
Salt, black pepper
Few sprigs rosemary
1 tsp. thyme

Heat broth and minced chicken, adding salt, pepper, rosemary and thyme. Meanwhile, make smooth paste with cornflour and ¼ cup cold water; add this to the heated broth, stirring constantly until mixture is thickened and translucent. Reduce heat and whisk in eggs, a little amount at a time, whisking constantly to separate the eggs into thin shreds. Remove from heat, add chopped spring onions, and serve.

MEATLESS EGG DROP SOUP

Spring being the season for plenty of eggs, here's another egg drop soup, this one using left-over fish— although chopped meat could be used in place of the fish if handier.

2 pts. stock
2 onions, sliced
1 cup (approx.) cooked flaked fish
4 Tbs. soya sauce
1 cup chopped spring onions
1 Tbs. cooking oil
3 eggs, beaten

Sauté onion in cooking oil in heavy saucepan. When transparent, add cooked fish and lightly brown. Now add soya sauce and stock. When just simmering, drop in egg mixture, a little at a time, whisking constantly to shred the egg. Continue cooking until egg is cooked.

Take off heat, add spring onions, and serve.

This was the first soup that Tony had in Singapore, and it is very delicious and surprisingly refreshing. It is often served with tiny dumplings (see pp 203-204) and is then almost a meal in itself.

CHICKEN SOUP, JEWISH STYLE

This is my favourite chicken soup, perhaps only because it brings back memories of my childhood. But it is very rich, and extremely delicious. The addition of the mint greatly alters the taste and, for me, the memory of the soup. Because when I was a child it was heavy with garlic, but no mint. But when living in Turkey, mint was always added to chicken soup—and I found it delicious, if different.

- 1 boiling chicken, including feet
- 5 pts. water
- 2 large carrots
- 2 large onions (or small bunch of spring onions, chopped)
- 1 small bunch parsley, finely chopped
- 3 cloves garlic, crushed
- 1 tsp. dried mint (optional)

Clean the chicken and its feet thoroughly. If you can get hold of extra feet, do! They make the soup extra rich.

Put chicken, feet and onions in a deep saucepan with water. Cook over medium heat, simmering gently, for about one-and-a-half hours. Add remaining ingredients except the garlic, and cook until the chicken is tender and falling off the bone—about another hour. Remove chicken and strain soup. Separate chicken from bones and return everything except the bones to the broth. Add crushed garlic. Serve with Cracker Balls (p.203).

CHICKEN AND BEAN SPROUT SOUP

Here's yet another soup using chicken, with a decidedly Eastern flavour. Directions for Sprouting Seeds on p. 219.

- 1 boiling chicken, plus feet or
- 3 pts. chicken broth
- 2 tsp. scraped ginger root
- 1 tsp. salt
- 3 tbs. oil
- 1 cup chopped spring onions
- 1 cup bean sprouts
- 3 hard-boiled eggs, sliced
- ½ cup chopped sorrel leaves for garnish.

Cook chicken with salt as in preceding recipe, strain, bone chicken, chop and return to broth. Heat oil in skillet, lightly cook onions, add sprouts, ginger and combine all with broth. Simmer, adding more salt or some soya sauce if desired, for a few minutes only. Serve at once, arranging slices of egg and some sorrel in each bowl.

THICK GREEN SOUP

Here's a good, basic recipe for using wild greens or thinnings from the garden.

- Approx. 1 lb. greens, washed and chopped (these can include thinnings, such as carrot, turnip, lettuce, raddish, etc., and wild foods such as nettles, chick pea or Good King Henry)
- 2 large onions, sliced
- 2 Tbs. cooking oil
- 2-3 pts. broth (or water with soya sauce: approx. 2 tsp. per pint of water)
- Left-over cereals (groats, wheat, barley)
- 1 large bay leaf
- 1 tsp. thyme
- Salt, black pepper

Sauté onion, salt, pepper, thyme and bay leaf in oil, until the onion is transparent. Add greens and cover tightly to cook for three to five minutes. Add broth, or water and soya sauce mixture, bring to simmering point, add cereals, cook a further few minutes and serve. Excellent served alongside dark homemade bread and cheese.

CREAMED GREEN SOUP

Here's another recipe for using up garden thinnings and wild foods. It's equally good, of course, made with spinach.

Approx. 1 lb of greens, as above, cooked and sieved or put through liquidiser
1 cup White Sauce (p. 199)
2-3 pts. fish, chicken or potato stock (or a mixture)
1 tsp. rosemary
Watercress to garnish

Mix together greens and stock and rosemary; gradually add to gently cooking white sauce, mixing all the time. Adjust the seasonings to taste. Sprinkle with paprika and garnish with watercress.

TURNIP THINNING SOUP

Finally, one more recipe for using up thinnings—this one is especially good for turnip thinnings, but can be made equally successfully with turnip tops in the summer, or those very old swede tops in the winter, as long as they are chopped well.

Approx. 2 cups cooked turnip thinnings
2 cups Cheese Sauce (p. 200)
2 cups stock (or water and soya sauce, as above)
2 cloves of garlic, crushed
Bay leaf
Salt, pepper

Sieve or liquidise turnip thinnings. Add to stock with salt, pepper, bay leaf and garlic. Add this mixture gently to the cheese sauce, stirring constantly. Adjust seasonings and serve garnished with chopped parsley or chopped sorrel.

THICK BROCCOLI STEM SOUP

Make this soup, saving the flowerets for salad (p. 58).

Bunch of thick broccoli stems, cut in ½-inch pieces
Butter
1 cup cooked, drained and washed barley or other cereal

1 onion, sliced
2 pts. (or more) potato water or vegetable stock
Salt, pepper, crushed garlic

Sauté broccoli, onion, seasonings in butter. When the broccoli is cooked (about ten to twelve minutes), add stock, simmer a few minutes and finally add the cooked cereal. This is a delicious, crunchy soup, both hearty and appetizing.

CREAM OF ASPARAGUS SOUP

We'll end with a party-piece soup—a little extravagant perhaps, but not unduly costly when made in spring, when all the ingredients are in season and plentiful.

1 lb. asparagus
3 pts. (approx.) potato peeling water
3 Tbs. butter
3 Tbs. flour
½ cup cream or milk
½ cup whipping cream
Salt, pepper, some grated nutmeg for garnish

Cut off about the top one-and-a-half inches from the asparagus and cook these tips in the soup stock with salt and pepper for about five minutes. Sieve the tips out and set aside. Now dice the stalks and cook these in the stock until tender. Put them through a sieve or liquidise.

Make sauce as follows:
Melt butter, gradually add flour, then 1 cup of the hot stock. Cook until smooth, adding liquidised or sieved stalks and remaining stock. When all blended, add the milk.

Serve immediately in bowls, topped with whipped cream and garnished with the asparagus tips and grated nutmeg.

MAIN COURSES

ASPARAGUS WITH BITTER ALMONDS

1 lb. asparagus
½ cup bitter almonds (hazel nuts can be substituted)
Generous pat of butter
Salt, freshly ground black pepper

Wash asparagus carefully, snapping off the lower tough stalks and removing the scales. Tie in bunches and place, with tips standing out of water, into a large amount of rapidly boiling salted water. After ten minutes, put lid on pot and cook further ten minutes to steam the tips. Take slivered almonds, roast in heavy skillet over flame until slightly browned, then brown a little further in melted butter. Pour over the cooked asparagus, sprinkle with freshly ground black pepper and serve at once. This is delicious served with an omelette and a savoury wheat or groats dish.

ASPARAGUS WITH HOT MAYONNAISE

1 lb. asparagus, cooked as above
½ cup White Sauce (p. 199)
1 cup Mayonnaise (pp. 198-9)
½ cup finely chopped sorrel or lemon balm—if you have some growing indoors for this is usually not available until summer

Cook the asparagus and set aside while combining, in saucepan, the white sauce and salad dressing. When hot, pour over the asparagus and garnish with the sorrel or lemon balm.

BROAD BEANS WITH BACON OR HAM

2 cups shelled broad beans
2 Tbs. butter
2 cups *Béchamel* Sauce (p. 199)
Some bacon or ham, cut into thin strips
1 Tbs. carraway seeds

Melt the butter in saucepan; add carraway seeds and cook until they start to pop. Add the shelled beans and a good pinch of salt, cover tightly and cook until just tender—about ten to fifteen minutes. Add a little water if you are afraid they will stick to the pan. Make the *béchamel*, add the bacon or ham, and pour over the hot beans. Excellent served with a plain cooked groats dish.

BAKED BROAD BEANS IN RELISH

This is a dish I remember from my childhood, but made with lima beans rather than broad beans. But this adaptation is delicious and hearty—and a meal in itself when served with a good, crusty hot homemade bread.

3 cups shelled broad beans
1 tsp. salt
1 cup Cucumber Relish (p. 149) or Tomato Relish (pp. 149-50) or a combination of the two
2 Tbs. melted butter or fat
1 large bay leaf

Cook the beans in small amount of salted water until just tender. Then, in a casserole, combine the melted butter, the beans, salt, the bay leaf and the relish. Bake in a medium to low oven for about one hour.

BROCCOLI

Broccoli is one of the most plentiful vegetables during spring. We grow lots in our garden and find it almost as versatile as the much maligned cabbage. Below are four of our favourite recipes.

ITALIAN STYLE BROCCOLI

2 good bunches of broccoli, or as much as you want to cook!
2 cloves of garlic—or as much or as little as you like
4 Tbs. (approx.) olive oil
Salt, black pepper freshly ground
½ cup sorrel leaves, chopped
Some salted cod—about ½ cup at least

Cut the broccoli into medium-sized pieces and cook in salted boiling water for ten minutes. Meanwhile, prepare the cod for cooking, and cook in the olive oil with the garlic. Add broccoli and a little water and cook until tender. Add freshly ground pepper and the sorrel leaves and serve very hot with some pasta (p. 205).

ORIENTAL STYLE BROCCOLI

1 or 2 bunches of broccoli
3 Tbs. oil
½ cup chopped spring onions
2 Tbs. soya sauce
2 Tbs. Red Wine (pp. 220-3)
Sprinkling of sugar
¼ cup boiling water

The broccoli should be crunchy for this dish, so do not over-cook. Cut the broccoli into bite-sized pieces. Heat oil in heavy skillet and sauté the broccoli and spring onions together for five minutes. Now mix the soya sauce, wine, sugar and boiling water and pour over the broccoli. Cover and cook for further five minutes. Serve with fried groats.

BROCCOLI—MACROBIOTIC STYLE

The following recipe, a *tempura* (which is a Japanese style of serving vegetables), is suitable for all sorts of vegetables, not just broccoli. It just so happens that we like broccoli done this way; but we also make it with cabbage, kale, root vegetables and even beetroot or carrot tops.

All you must remember is to cut your vegetables into handy pieces and remember that leafy ones only need a few minutes cooking while the root vegetables, preferably cut into strips, take a little longer. As your vegetables are done, put them to drain on a piece of brown paper in a low oven—this will keep them crisp and warm while you are finishing the other vegetables, and you can then serve them at once, giving each person a teacup with a little dip in it. Eat the tempura with your fingers. It's delicious and isn't half as much trouble as it looks. For a start, the dip can be made hours ahead, and the same with the batter.

Cut the broccoli into handy-sized pieces and set aside in a cool place while preparing the batter.

Batter:

½ cup brown flour
½ cup white flour
1 egg
1 cup water
1 teaspoon salt

Add the dry ingredients to the wet and whisk lightly. Do not over-beat as it makes the batter heavy and sticky. And don't worry about any lumps. Chill for a while before using.

Heat oil for frying using a deep saucepan. When the oil is very hot, take the broccoli pieces and dip into the batter, thoroughly coating them, and quickly place into the hot oil. The vegetables will sink to the bottom at first, and as they cook rise to the top. Turn over to get both sides a lovely golden brown. (Don't over-crowd the saucepan as it will only cause the vegetables to stick together and not cook.)

When all are done, serve at once with the following dip:

1 piece of ginger root, grated, or
½ tsp. of ground ginger
1½ cups water
½ cup tahini (ground sesame product)
½ cup chopped spring onions

Mix all the ingredients together, being careful to keep it smooth. Let stand to blend the flavours before serving with the tempura.

BROCCOLI WITH CHEESE SAUCE AND NUTS

Cook the broccoli as above, in the Italian-style recipe, and serve with cheese sauce (p. 200) to which chopped hazelnuts or walnuts have been added. Serve with a fried groats or a wheat dish which has been flavoured with thyme and a little rosemary.

BOREK

'Borek' is a dish found all over the Middle East—it is rolled filled pastry which is flaky and crackly, and absolutely delicious. Traditionally, the pastry, *file*, is bought in specialist shops but we find that puff pastry, rolled out as thin as possible, does quite well (pp. 207-8).

Roll out the pastry thinly, in a circle, cut into wedges (as you'd cut a pie), each wedge about three or four inches at the outer edge. Place a spoonful of any of the fillings given below at the outer edge, and roll each wedge inwards. It should be thin, like your finger. Fry in very hot deep oil and serve drained, with a large hearty salad.

Fillings:

GOAT'S CHEESE

½ lb. Goat's Cheese, crumbled (pp. 216-18)
1 egg
Good pinch oregano
Black pepper, ground
A little oil

Crumble the goat's cheese and add the egg and other ingredients, mixing well.

CROWDIE

1 cup Crowdie (p. 216)
2 cloves garlic, crushed
Salt, pepper
1 cup of chopped thinnings from the garden (any thinnings will do—lettuce, carrot, turnip, beet, etc.)
or
1 cup chopped spring onions
or
1 cup parsley

Combine, mixing well.

MINCED MEAT

½ lb. minced meat (beef or mutton)
1 egg
1 teaspoon ground cummin
Good pinch dried mint
Salt and pepper

Combine all ingredients and mix well.

SPRING CABBAGE AND SAUSAGE (OR WITH STUFFED HELZEL, p. 48)

8-12 sausages
Black pepper, ground
Grated nutmeg
Good quantity spring cabbage, roughly chopped

Cook the sausages until crisp and brown. Take from pan and pour off all but about three to four tablespoons of the fat. Place the cabbage in the fat and cook until tender but not soggy, stirring well. Arrange in a hot dish with thyme-seasoned wheat and garnished with the sausages. Grate the nutmeg over all. Sprinkle with the pepper. Delicious served with any pickled vegetables like turnips, carrots, cucumbers. (See p. 00.)

SPRING CABBAGE WITH DILL

Lightly sauté in butter some chopped onion and a good amount of dill seed. When the onions are soft, add salt, chopped spring cabbage and cook a further ten minutes. Serve with groats and a side dish of yoghurt, on which black pepper has been freshly ground.

Chicken

As stated in the soup section, spring is a good time for chicken dishes. Since chicken is also popular in the Orient, many of the recipes below are adaptations of dishes Tony has had on his travels from Australia to Britain.

But I will begin with instructions on how to render fat from a chicken (or, incidentally, a goose). The resulting fat is excellent for cooking vegetables, and as a child I would have it spread thinly on dark bread, sprinkled with coarse salt!

When cleaning your chicken, remove all fat and fatty skins. Wash and drain this and cut into small pieces. Cook over low heat until the fat is almost melted. Now, for each cup of fat to be rendered you'll need one sliced onion and a quarter of an apple, chopped. Add the onions and apple to the fat and cook until the onions are brown. Be careful not to burn them—use a very low flame. Cook and strain the fat, setting aside the onion and pieces of skin (cracklings) which can be kept in a cool place and used in any seasoned wheat or groat dishes.

CHICKEN CURRY

- 1 large, or 2 small, chickens, jointed (save the giblets and feet for soups)
- 3 tsp. curry powder
- 2 Tbs. soya sauce
- 3 cloves garlic, crushed
- 1 tsp. chili peppers, ground
- 4 Tbs. oil
- 1 stick or 2 tsp. ground cinnamon
- 3 bay leaves
- Salt to taste

Wash and dry the chicken parts and rub into each a mixture of the curry powder and soya sauce. Heat the oil in a deep, heavy skillet and lightly cook the chili peppers; then add chicken and cover with the water and the rest of the ingredients. Cook over low heat for about an hour. Serve with wheat to which chopped raw onion is added.

CHICKEN AND FRIED GROATS

- 2 cups groats, uncooked
- 1 boiling chicken
- 4 Tbs. oil
- 4 onions, sliced
- 3 garlic cloves, crushed
- 1 tsp. cummin
- 1 scant tsp. ground chili peppers (can be omitted)
- 1 tsp. coriander
- ½ cup hazelnuts
- 4 Tbs. peanut butter

Cook chicken, feet and all, until meat falls from bone. Strain and separate meat from bones. Set meat aside. Cook the groats in the chicken water; when cooked, rinse well.

Heat oil in large saucepan and sauté the onions with some salt, and the coriander. When the coriander starts to pop, stir in the groats, and cook until browned. Finally, add the rest of the ingredients, stirring to keep from sticking, and cook a further ten minutes.

Excellent served with a green salad.

SPICED CHICKEN WITH NOODLES

When we lived in Devonshire we learned the delights of cooking with sharp apple cider. The following is a superb recipe for any celebration.

- 2 chickens, jointed
- ½ cup oil
- 4 cloves garlic, minced
- 1 good-sized ginger root, grated or 4 tsp. ginger
- 2 Tbs. curry powder
- 2 pts. cider
- 3 Tbs. cornflour
- Hard-boiled eggs and watercress for garnish
- 6 cups cooked, drained, flat Noodles (p. 205)

Heat oil in deep, heavy skillet and sauté the garlic, ginger and curry powder for about five minutes, stirring to keep from sticking. Add chicken parts and cook a further ten to fifteen minutes. Now sprinkle on the salt and then add one pint of the cider. Cover and cook for about thirty to forty-five minutes—until the chicken is tender.

Meanwhile, mix the cornflour with a few spoonfuls of the cider into a smooth paste. Blend this into the rest of the cider and add, stirring well, to the chicken and sauce. Cook until the sauce has thickened.

Serve over noodles garnished with the egg and cress, and with a green salad to which lots of chopped spring onion has been added.

CHICKEN AND FRIED WHEAT

- 3 cups cooked wheat
- 4 Tbs. butter
- 1 cup cooked chicken (This can be reserved from the soup recipe, or can be left-over roasted chicken, cut up; bacon, ham and sausage can also be used, singly or in combination.)
- 1 cup chopped spring onions
- 2 eggs, beaten
- ½ cup chopped parsley
- ½ cup Bean Sprouts (p. 219)
- 2-3 Tbs. soya sauce
- Salt, pepper to taste

Heat the butter in heavy skillet and cook wheat in it to brown slightly. Add the chicken (or other meat), spring onions, salt and pepper, and cook a few minutes, stirring constantly.

With the back of a wooden spoon make a hollow in the middle of the mixture and pour the beaten egg into it. Stir well until it gets milky, then mix into the entire wheat mixture. When ready to serve, add the parsley, soya sauce and the bean sprouts; cook just to heat—about one minute—and serve with a side dish of yoghurt.

I'll end the chicken recipes with an old Eastern European recipe for Stuffed Helzel. These can be made as the ingredients are available and stored in the freezer until you have enough to fry up and serve with mashed potatoes and a crisp green salad.

STUFFED HELZEL

When preparing your chicken for any of the above recipes, carefully remove the neck skin and sew together one end of it with ordinary thread and needle. Stuff with the following mixture and sew up the other end. Fry whole but cut into slices to serve.

¾ cup brown flour
1 Tbs. grated onion
2 Tbs. rendered chicken fat (see above)
Salt, pepper, paprika to taste

Mix all ingredients together, rubbing fat well into flour. Fill the neck skin and sew up.

Cheese

With the coming of the green grass, our recently kidded goats munch steadily and give us plenty of milk. This is the season when we start making cheeses and in the back of the book are a few recipes for goat's and cow's milk cheeses. Below are a few recipes in which cheese plays the main part.

CHEESE AND WHEAT CASSEROLE

3 cups grated carrots
2 cups cooked wheat
2 eggs, beaten
1 medium-sized onion, grated
Salt, freshly ground black pepper
Good pinch thyme
½ cup yoghurt or milk to which 1 tsp. vinegar has been added to sour
2 cups grated Cheddar cheese

Combine the carrots, wheat, egg, yoghurt (or soured milk), seasonings, onion and 1½ cups of the cheese. Mix thoroughly and pat into a greased casserole. Sprinkle with the remaining cheese and bake in a moderate oven for about thirty to forty-five minutes.

Serve with pickled vegetables (especially good with Pickled Cabbage, (pp. 145-6) or a crunchy green salad.

CHEDDAR CRÊPES

1 cup plain flour
1 tsp. salt
6 eggs, beaten
3 cups milk (sour milk can be used, or 2 tsp. of vinegar can be added to sweet milk to sour it)
3 Tbs. melted butter
½ cup grated Cheddar cheese
Butter for pan

Sift the flour and salt into bowl and stir in the beaten eggs. Add milk slowly, whisking gently; then add the melted butter and finally the cheese. The batter should be quite smooth and it is best to leave it to stand for an hour before using it.

Heat pan and melt some butter in it. When it is almost smoking, pour about two or three tablespoons of batter in. Swirl it around to cover the bottom of the pan quickly, then turn. It only takes about a minute on each side, so move quickly! When the crêpe is done, flip it onto a plate. Butter the pan between each crêpe or the cheese will make it stick. When all the crêpes are done, roll them up and place in a buttered baking dish. Cover with a slightly damp tea towel and heat the crêpes for about ten minutes in a moderate oven. Serve with either a *béchamel* sauce thick with parsley or cress, or with a dark Mushroom Sauce (p. 200).

CHEESE AND SPRING ONION PIE

Puff Pastry for lining of dish (pp. 207-8)
1 cup spring onions, chopped
1 Tbs. of butter
1 cup Cheddar cheese, cubed
3 eggs, beaten
1½ cups light cream
Grated nutmeg
Pinch of mace
Salt and pepper

Roll out puff pastry and line pie dish with it. Prick and bake in a pre-heated hot oven (450°F) for about five minutes while you prepare the filling.

Melt butter in pan and gently sauté the spring onions. Sprinkle this on the bottom of the crust. On top put the cubed Cheddar cheese.

Mix the eggs with the cream and seasoning and blend well. Pour over the spring onions and cheese, and bake for about fifteen minutes in hot oven. Now turn down the heat to medium (350°F) and bake another ten to fifteen minutes, or until an inserted knife comes out clean. Can be served either hot or cold, and delicious either way.

DANDELION LEAVES SAUTÉD IN GARLIC

We use cultivated dandelion leaves, which are not ready until the summer. But the wild dandelion come up fresh and tender in the spring which is the best time to pick them, before the milky juices start to rise and the leaves become bitter.

2 lb. fresh leaves	Oil
Small bunch spring onions, chopped	Salt and freshly ground black pepper
3 cloves garlic, crushed	

Wash the leaves and cut them in half. Cook the spring onions in oil; add garlic and finally the dandelion leaves, salt and pepper. Cook for ten minutes, or until tender, and serve on toast. The addition of some mushrooms (along with the spring onions) is very good.

Eggs

Eggs are plentiful this time of year, which is why many of the recipes are rich in eggs. But below are some special egg recipes which we like preparing at this time of year, after the winter's scarcity of eggs.

EGG CURRY

4 Tbs. butter	1 Tbs. tomato paste
1 onion, sliced	1½ cups milk
1 clove garlic, minced	1 tsp. salt
1 tsp. dill seed	6 eggs, hard-boiled and cut lengthwise
1 Tbs. curry powder	

Melt butter in skillet; sauté onion, garlic, dill seed for five minutes. Blend in curry powder and tomato paste and stir constantly for one minute. Gradually add the milk, stirring steadily till all is blended. Cook over low heat for ten minutes. Add salt and eggs, and serve over cooked and drained groats.

EGG ROLLS

Pancakes:

2 eggs, beaten	good pinch of salt
½ cup milk, soured with drop of vinegar	½ cup flour
	1 Tbs. oil

Beat eggs, milk and salt together, then beat into this the flour. Heat the oil in skillet and pour two to three tablespoons of batter into skillet, swirling around to spread, and cook until browned on bottom (bubbles will appear on top) and take out. These are cooked only on one side as they will be fried with the filling later. Stack the cooked pancakes and prepare the filling.

Filling:

- 1 cup chopped spring onions, or a combination of spring onion and ordinary chopped onions.
- 1 cup chopped spring cabbage or collards
- 1 cup thinnings or finely chopped tops of parsnips, or hamburg parsley which have begun to grow again.
- Salt, pepper
- Good pinch celery seed
- 2 Tbs. oil

Cook all the greens and onions in oil for about five minutes then add salt, pepper and celery seed. Some left-over meat can be chopped and added at this stage.

Place one heaped tablespoon of the filling at one end of the pancake, browned side up, and roll up, tucking in the ends. Seal with a little beaten egg and chill. The chilling is important as otherwise the egg rolls will fall apart in the frying (which makes this an excellent recipe to prepare well before guests arrive).

Heat oil in deep saucepan until it is almost smoking and pop in a few of the rolls at a time. They will not take more than a few minutes to brown nicely on the outside. Stack on brown paper in a low oven while the rest are frying.

This will make about six nice-sized pancakes and is delicious served with a hot Mustard Sauce (p. 199).

EGG AND GREEN PIE

- 2 lb. fresh nettles, chickweed, dandelion or spinach (or any greens available)
- 4 Tbs. oil
- 6 eggs
- Salt and pepper
- Butter
- ½ cup grated Cheddar cheese
- 1½ cups *Béchamel* Sauce (p. 199)
- Puff Pastry for lining dish (pp. 207-8)

Line dish with puff pastry, prick and bake in hot oven for about five minutes while you prepare greens by roughly chopping them and cooking them in the heated oil until they are just wilted. Season with salt and pepper and stir so that all the leaves are coated with oil.

Take out the lined pie dish and spread the cooked greens on it. With the back of a spoon make six hollows in the greens and pour a little melted butter into each hollow. Carefully break an egg in each and sprinkle the grated cheese over each one. Now pour over the sauce and bake in a medium oven for about fifteen minutes.

EGG KUGEL

Sometime in the Middle Ages, *kugels*, or puddings, became an important part of Jewish cooking. The following *kugel* is savoury and can be served hot or cold.

- 6 eggs, separated
- 3 cups minced onions and spring onions
- ½ cup crumbled water biscuits
- 2 tsp. salt
- Ground black pepper
- 4 Tbs. melted butter (or rendered chicken fat)

Beat egg yolks until thick and lemony-yellow. Stir in the onions, crumbled biscuits, salt, pepper and butter (or fat). Fold in stiffly-beaten egg whites and turn into well greased large casserole. Bake for forty-five minutes in a moderate oven, until inserted knife comes out clean.

MIDDLE-EASTERN EGGS

- 6 eggs, hard-boiled and shelled
- 2 Tbs. butter
- Seasoning mixture:
  - a good pinch each of salt
  - black pepper
  - ground cummin
  - paprika

Prick the egg whites with a fork all over and cook the eggs, turning frequently, in the hot butter in a shallow pan over a medium heat. When the eggs are slightly browned, roll them in the seasoning mixture.

Serve hot with seasoned wheat or groats in which a good handful of watercress or parsley has been chopped.

EGG FOO YUNG

6 eggs
1 cup chopped onion
1 cup bean sprouts
1 cup flaked white fish
3 tsp. soya sauce
Pepper
Oil for frying

Whisk eggs until frothy; add rest of ingredients and mix well with fork. Heat oil in heavy skillet. Pour mixture by ladlefuls (or about ½ teacupful) into skillet; let brown on both sides. Keep omelettes warm whilst preparing the following sauce:

2 cups chicken broth or vegetable water
2 Tbs. cornflour
3 tsp. treacle
2 tsp. soya sauce

Combine cornflour into a paste with a little of the liquid; mix in saucepan with remaining liquid, adding treacle and soya sauce, and cook until thick.

Pour over omelettes and serve.

BROCCOLI OMELETTE

Another omelette, but this with a definite Italian flavour and delicious served with homemade bread.

1 bunch broccoli
6 eggs
4 Tbs. olive oil
2 cloves garlic, crushed
6 Tbs. grated Cheddar cheese (or some salty crumbled goat's cheese)
Salt and black pepper to taste

Let the broccoli stand in cold water a little while to become crisp. Split stalks and cook broccoli in rapidly boiling salted water until tender—ten to fifteen minutes only. Drain and cut in small pieces.

Beat eggs thoroughly in large bowl and add the rest of the ingredients, and finally the broccoli. Mix well. Heat oil in heavy skillet and pour in mixture. Cook until puffy and browned on one side. Turn carefully and brown on other side.

NETTLES, SAUTÉD

Wash and chop the nettles and sauté in butter in which sliced onion has been cooked. Add salt, pepper, minced garlic and a tablespoon or two of home-brew beer (or whatever beer you're drinking!). Serve with a white sauce sprinkled with paprika.

NETTLES, COOKED

Wash and finely chop nettles. Cook a few minutes only in rapidly boiling salted water. Heat some butter in a skillet and sauté an onion in it. Add some breadcrumbs, salt, pepper, some grated nutmeg and a little stock or some of the water from the nettles. Add the chopped nettles. Delicious served with hard-boiled eggs, or Middle-Eastern eggs with wheat or groats.

NETTLE SOUFFLÉ

2 Tbs. oil
2 Tbs. flour
¼ cup water
4 eggs separated
1½ cups cooked nettles (or other greens), sieved or put through the blender

Heat skillet, add oil and when hot, blend in the flour. Cool the skillet and blend flour very well, stirring in the egg yolks. Now add the sieved or blended greens (squeeze out excess moisture). Whisk egg whites until stiff but not dry. Carefully fold into spinach mixture and quickly pour this mixture into a straight-sided baking dish which has been dusted with flour. Place immediately in an oven pre-heated to 375°F and bake for about forty-five minutes, or until nicely browned and puffed. The secret of a soufflé is to do it quickly, and serve it immediately once it is out of the oven.

HAMBURG PARSLEY

This is generally regarded as a winter vegetable but it stands well and we use it in the spring when vegetables are still scarce.

Save the greens for relish or soup. Scrub the roots and split them down the centre, sprinkling with sesame seeds, salt and pepper. Cook in a little butter, adding more sesame seeds if desired. Garnish with chopped spring onions and serve with savoury wheat or groats.

PARSNIP PATTIES

Parsnips too, are generally regarded as winter vegetables but also stand well.

Scrub roots and cook in boiling salted water until tender—about thirty to forty-five minutes. Drain, plunge in cold water to slip off their skins. Wash and season with butter, salt and pepper. Shape into round flat cakes, roll in flour, and fry in butter or other fat until crisp and brown.

Last season's carrots are good treated this way also.

SEAKALE

Cook lightly in salted water and serve with melted butter in which some nuts have been browned. Or serve on toast with a sauce of your choice.

SEAKALE BEET

Take ribs and cook like asparagus (p. 40) and serve with a cheese sauce.

The greens can be treated like spinach or used in any of the above recipes calling for greens.

WHEAT PANCAKES

2 cups pre-cooked wheat
2 eggs, beaten
½ cup oatmeal
1 teaspoon of ground cummin
Butter (or oil) for frying

Approx. ¾ cup wholemeal flour—enough to thicken batter and make it a little firm
Salt, freshly ground black pepper

Grated carrots, potatoes, parsnips, can be part-substituted for some of the wheat.

Place wheat in bowl; add beaten eggs and mix well. Add oatmeal and enough flour to bind mixture. Season. Drop by spoonfuls onto griddle or into heavy skillet in which butter or oil has been heated. Turn when crinkled at edges. Keep finished pancakes warm in low oven whilst frying the remainder. Serve with Yoghurt (pp. 200 and 218), Cheese Sauce (p. 200), pickles, chutney, or relish.

Chopped thinnings can be added along with the wheat for variation.

ROAST LEG OF SPRING LAMB WITH DILL

In many rural areas of the world roast lamb has been traditionally prepared to celebrate the arrival of guests, and as such has a ritual significance probably not unconnected with the idea of sacrifice. We may not make sacrifices anymore, but it mightn't be a bad idea to reserve this dish for a special feast occasion, and then to cook it with all the care it deserves. The first time we had this was in Turkey. The lamb had been killed especially for us and, I must admit, at first I thought this would put me off. But the care and joy with which this was served was so quietly beautiful that the dish always had a very special significance for us.

1 large leg of lamb
2 large onions, sliced
4-5 cloves of garlic, slivered
4 tsp. fresh dillweed if available, or 2 tsp. dried dillweed
2 Tbs. olive oil
Salt, freshly-ground black pepper

Wipe lamb clean and cut off all excess fat. Make tiny slits all over the leg with the point of a sharp knife, and insert the slivers of garlic. Rub leg well with olive oil, then rub into it the salt, pepper, and dillweed.

Place in ovenproof dish, surrounded by the sliced onion. Cover and cook two to three hours in moderate oven, turning every now and then.

This is delicious served with groats which have been browned in a little of the lamb roasting oil, and with a large crunchy salad on the side.

SALADS

BROCCOLI HEAD AND NEW CARROT SALAD

These new carrots are just too good to cook. Much better to cut them into sticks and combine with raw broccoli flowerettes (the stems saved for soup, p. 58) and tossed in a Toasted Sesame Dressing (p. 198).

CAULIFLOWER AND TOASTED NUT DRESSING

Take cauliflower flowerettes (stalks and leaves can be used in soup or chopped into Wheat Pancakes, pp. 56-7) and toss well in a Toasted Seed Dressing (p. 198). Cubes of Cheddar cheese and a little chopped pickled vegetable go well also.

CORN SALAD AND SORREL

Wash leaves and add very thinly sliced onion. Toss in a French dressing. Excellent with sliced hard-boiled egg.

DANDELION AND EARLY LETTUCE SALAD

Wash and separate leaves; add sliced early radishes and perhaps some early carrots too. Toss in a Stilton Cheese Dressing (p. 197).

SUBSTANTIAL SALADS

If you still have some root vegetables, grate any combination of these (black or red winter radishes; Hamburg parsley; parsnip, carrots) and combine with chopped watercress or American cress, perhaps some cubed Cheddar cheese and hard-boiled eggs. Pour over a light Mayonnaise Dressing (pp. 198-9) and serve with hot homebaked bread.

DESSERTS

Rhubarb is the most available fruit in spring—especially in early spring when there is precious little else available, except perhaps some Newton Wonder cooking apples. So I'll start by giving recipes which offer a variety of ways of using rhubarb, both by itself or in combination.

RHUBARB PIE

Boil about one pound of rhubarb in water with sugar to taste. When tender, strain off juice (save for jelly, recipe below), add a cupful of dried fruit (raisins, currants, etc.) and some mixed spice.

Line pie dish with pastry (pp. 206-7), put in the rhubarb and raisin mixture, and cover with more pastry. Prick top and bake until brown—about twenty minutes in a hot oven. (If the edges threaten to darken too much, cover with a little tin foil.)

RHUBARB JELLY

For every pint of rhubarb cooking water add half an ounce gelatine and stir until dissolved. Pour into mould and let set. Serve with spiced cookies, p. 61.

BAKED RHUBARB

Wash and cut rhubarb. Place in baking dish, dot with butter and sprinkle with a mixture of cinnamon and sugar. Cover and bake for about forty-five minutes in a medium oven. The rhubarb will be a lovely red colour and is delicious served with any variation of the butter cookies given below.

SPICED RHUBARB

Wash, wipe and cut up rhubarb (about half a pound or one pound) and arrange into a well-buttered pie dish. Sprinkle liberally with sugar (preferably brown).

Make batter as follows:

Sieve into bowl about one-and-a-half cups of flour and a pinch of salt. Make a well in the centre and drop in two eggs (or only one if you're feeling mean!) and enough milk to make a batter. Mix well and finally add one teaspoon each of mixed spice and ginger. Pour over the rhubarb and bake in a hot oven until brown and crisp. Can be served hot or cold.

RHUBARB AND APPLE CRUMBLE

In well-buttered, deep, ovenproof dish arrange cut-up rhubarb and apple. Over the top liberally sprinkle the following *streusel*:

- 4 Tbs. butter
- 4 Tbs. flour
- 4 Tbs. brown sugar
- 1 tsp. cinnamon
- Some grated almonds, hazelnuts, or walnuts

Mix all the ingredients together well by rubbing with the finger tips until small crumbs are formed. Bake crumble in a medium oven for about forty-five minutes. Great served on its own, or with ice cream if it's handy.

BASIC RECIPE FOR BUTTER COOKIES

All cookies below are to be baked in pre-heated 400°F oven, on ungreased baking trays.

- 1 cup butter
- 1½ cups icing sugar
- 1½ cups sifted flour
- 1 egg
- 1 tsp. cream of tartar
- 1 tsp. baking soda
- 1 tsp. vanilla
- Pinch of salt

Cream butter and add the sugar gradually, beating until light and fluffy. Add egg and vanilla and beat well. Sift together the dry ingredients and blend into creamed mixture.

ROLLED CRISPIES

Chill the dough, then roll out on floured board as thin as possible (about 1/8 inch). Cut with floured cutters and bake for five minutes. Half this recipe makes about three dozen.

ANISE BALLS

To half the above dough add about half a cup ground walnuts or hazelnuts and one tablespoon ground anise. Chill well. Roll dough into balls the size of walnuts and bake about eight to ten minutes. When done, roll at once in some icing sugar, and again when cool. Makes about two dozen.

SESAME SEED ROUNDS

Form half of the dough into a roll about two inches in diameter and wrap in greaseproof paper. Chill until firm. Slice thinly (1/8 inch) if possible. Brush the tops with milk and sprinkle with sesame seeds. Bake about five minutes. Makes about three dozen.

SPICED COOKIES

To half the dough add two tablespoons of treacle (or molasses, which is better if you have it), scant teaspoon of ginger, one teaspoon of cinnamon and some grated nutmeg. Roll out to 1/8 inch thickness and cut into patterns. Bake about five minutes. Will make three dozen.

The variations for the above dough are endless—limited only by ingredients at hand and your own imagination. We roll balls of the dough in dessicated coconut, sugar and cinnamon, brush the tops with beaten egg yolk and sprinkle on nuts or various seeds, and ice the baked shapes with a thin glaze made of icing sugar, a drop of colouring and a little water; and add cocoa powder and even instant coffee powder to the dough before shaping it.

APPLE FRITTERS

2 eggs, beaten	1 cup flour
Pinch of salt	Good pinch of cinnamon
¾ cup water or cold herbal tea	2 medium cooking apples

Beat the eggs, salt and water or tea together; add to the flour and mix well. Peel, core and chop the apples and combine with the cinnamon, and finally with the flour mixture, blending well. Heat oil for frying, and drop fritter mixture in by tablespoons. Fry until golden brown, drain, and serve hot with a dusting of icing sugar.

LAYERED CHOCOLATE AND VANILLA PUDDING

4 Tbs. cornflour	¼ cup cold milk
2 Tbs. unsweetened cocoa powder	1 pt. milk, scalded
	1 tsp. vanilla
Pinch of salt	4 egg whites, beaten stiff

Combine cornflour, cocoa, and salt and make a smooth paste with the cold milk. Add to the scalded milk and place in double boiler (or if you are using a kitchen range just cook in an ordinary saucepan on the cooler part) and cook for about fifteen minutes, stirring constantly, while the mixture thickens. Set aside while preparing the vanilla custard:

1 pt. hot milk	½ teaspoon vanilla or almond flavouring
4 egg yolks	
¼ cup sugar	

Beat egg yolks slightly, add sugar and a pinch of salt. Place in double boiler (or if using a range, cook as above) and stir constantly while beating in the hot milk. When the mixture thickens and will coat the spoon, take off heat and add the flavouring. Set aside.

Now add the flavouring to the chocolate pudding and fold in the stiffly beaten egg whites.

Butter a glass serving dish and crumble some Digestive Biscuits (p. 63) on the bottom. Pour about half of the vanilla or almond custard in, then another layer of crumbled biscuits, one-third of the chocolate pudding, another layer of biscuits, and so on, until the pudding is used up. Refrigerate or let stand in a cool place for twelve hours or so. You should then be able to cut it into squares and serve—with whipped cream if you like.

CARAMELISED BAKED BOSTON CUSTARD

Make this in small round glass baking dishes for lovely individual puddings. Take four quarter-pint glasses (or one large glass baking dish) and pour into each a little melted butter; now put about one tablespoon of sugar in each and brown in the oven, tilting the dishes so they are evenly coated.

Make the custard as follows:

1 pt. hot milk	Pinch of salt
2 eggs	Grated nutmeg to taste
4 Tbs. sugar	

Beat the eggs slightly, add salt and sugar and stir until the sugar dissolves. Pour milk gradually over the eggs and add the grated nutmeg. Pour into the buttered and sugared glasses and place them in a pan of hot water and bake for twenty to thirty minutes in a moderate (350°F) oven. Test: if an inserted knife comes out clean, they're done. To serve, invert glasses onto dish—custard should slip out.

If you're baking this in a large pudding dish, just place the the dish in the oven and bake as above.

DIGESTIVE BISCUITS

1 cup oatmeal	1 cup butter
1 cup wholewheat flour	Pinch of salt
1 cup brown sugar	Pinch of bicarb. of soda

Cream butter and sugar together; add flour, oatmeal and salt and soda. Sprinkle surface liberally with oatmeal and roll out; sprinkle a little oatmeal on top also and roll this gently in. Cut into rounds and bake in a buttered tin in a fairly hot (400°F) oven. Much better than the bought variety.

CHEESECAKE WITH WINE GLAZE

This is another very rich, very delicious cake using Crowdie. New York has some delicious cheesecakes and I understand that they fly them over to London now. Ridiculous when you can make them yourself and be sure that the cake you get is made with the best of ingredients, without costing a fortune. This one with a wine glaze we use for very special occasions—one of the children insisting it be her birthday cake.

For the crust you will need:

1½ cups digestive biscuit crumbs	¼ cup brown sugar
	¼ cup butter, melted

Mix the sugar and crumbs, blend in the butter. Press this mixture evenly on the bottom and sides of a greased cake tin.

For the filling you will need:

4 eggs, separated	½ cup raisins
½ cup sugar	1 tsp. cinnamon
3 cups Crowdie (p. 216)	Grated nutmeg
Pinch of salt	

Mix thoroughly the cheese, sugar, salt and beaten egg yolks. Add raisins; fold in stiffly-beaten egg whites and spices.

Pour mixture into the lined cake dish and bake for ten minutes in pre-heated hot oven (400°F). Reduce heat (or place cake on lower rack in oven) to 350°F and cook for a further half-hour or until inserted knife comes out clean.

For the glaze you will need:

1 cup Red Wine (pp. 221-3)
1 Tbs. cornflour

Make a smooth paste with the cornflour and some of the red wine then combine rest of wine and cook until thickened over a gentle heat. Arrange some nuts or raisins or glacé cherries on top of the cake, pour the glaze over and let set. Keep cake overnight in fridge or a cool place to let all the flavours blend and to ensure it will slice nicely.

GINGER CHEESECAKE WITH YOGHURT

A delicious cheesecake, not as rich as the one above, and with a more tangy taste, but definitely to be served on special occasions.

Sweet Shortcrust recipe (pp. 206-7)
2 cups Crowdie (p. 216)
½ cup sugar
1 Tbs. freshly grated ginger root
2 eggs

Make the pastry as directed, and pre-bake.

Meanwhile, mix together, blending until smooth, the Crowdie, sugar, eggs, and ginger. Pour into baked pie shell. Return to oven and bake at 350°F for about twenty to twenty-five minutes.

For the topping combine the following:

1 cup yoghurt (pp. 218-9)
¼ cup sugar
2 Tbs. crystallised ginger, slivered

Spread the topping on the cheesecake, and return to the oven (which you've since turned off) for just a few minutes. Now chill well (overnight, as in above recipe, is best).

RELISHES, CHUTNEYS, PICKLES

It's a good idea to make these when the relevant foods are at their most abundant and cheapest. I find that each season has some foods worth preserving for condiments, and the following are three very basic recipes for spring. I also store large amounts in glass sweet jars which you can buy for about 10p each.

BASIC GREEN RELISH

6 lb. fresh greens (including thinnings from the garden, young nettle and burdock, chickweed, carrot and beetroot tops)
1 cup brown sugar
½ pt. vinegar
½ cup cummin seed
6 large bay leaves
3 thick sticks cinnamon
¼ cup coriander seed
1 Tbs. cloves
Salt

Wash and chop the greens finely. As you fill a large cooking pot with the choppings, salt well. When pot is full, add sugar, vinegar and the spices. Bring to boil and keep at the boil, with the lid off to let excess moisture escape, for about twenty to thirty minutes. If your pot is too small to hold all the greens at one go, put in as many as the pot will hold, add remaining ingredients and the rest of the greens as the mixture boils down. When the relish is thoroughly cooked (but not mushy) take off heat and pour into clean hot jars. Cool and then seal.

This is ready for use immediately but, of course, is much better if kept for some weeks or months. The cummin and coriander gives it a Middle-Eastern flavour which goes well with minced meat and cheese dishes.

BROCCOLI SPEARS IN BRINE

Last April I found that my late purple sprouting broccoli was giving more shoots than our family could cope with. Not only that, but Tony wanted to pull up the plants and put in some salad greens for the summer. But we kept putting it off because the plants kept sprouting more and more shoots. Suddenly, inspiration! I'd never heard of pickled broccoli, but there's always a first time. Since I wasn't sure how it would work, I decided to use a simple brine solution. It was delicious and we are now planting extra broccoli just so that we can pickle some for winter use.

Brine:

1 cup coarse salt to 5 cups of water (or enough to float a fresh egg)

Pack cut-up broccoli (heads should be whole, but the stems and leaves should be cut up into one-inch pieces) in clean jars. Arrange slivered garlic cloves and fresh dillweed (if available) along with the broccoli. Pour over the brine solution to completely cover the broccoli. If some persists in sticking up, place a large cabbage or burdock leaf over the top, weighting it down with a clean stone. Just make sure no broccoli sticks up.

Keep in a warm place—but out of the sunlight—for about ten days or until all fermentation stops. If some scum rises to the top, skim it off. When the pickles are done, it is best to put them into clean jars and cover with fresh brine. Done this way the broccoli can keep for up to a year.

Incidentally, carrots, turnips, beets and cauliflower can be preserved the same way. Cucumbers are also good, but we prefer them with a little vinegar.

RHUBARB CHUTNEY

1 lb. chopped rhubarb
2 onions, sliced
½ cup chopped spring onions
2 teaspoons curry powder
1 tsp. cinnamon
1 tsp. mustard
1 tsp. salt
½ tsp. cayenne pepper
3 Tbs. brown sugar
½ cup (or more) Vinegar (pp. 196-7)

Place all the ingredients in a pot and cook slowly until rhubarb is soft. Then boil rapidly for a few minutes to agitate the flavour together, adding more vinegar as necessary. Cool and pour into clean warm jars. Seal.

This chutney keeps extremely well and makes lovely Christmas gifts if packed into decorative jars.

JAM

Chapter Three
Summer

SOUPS

Summer is the time for cold soups, so in this section we've included all we know. For those with blenders the variety of flavours, if not textures, is endless. For those without blenders or, indeed, for those few like us who have willingly refused the electricity rat race, shunning that power source altogether, cold soup making is perhaps more work but the results are, if different, just as delicious. And after all, our point in putting together this book is to show that we *can* reduce our reliance on foreign foodstuffs and extravagant natural resources without losing in the variety and joy of tastes. What is more, we gain in the genuine excitement of cooking which is much too happy and creative a task to shove willy nilly at the ever-increasing array of kitchen gadgets we seem to be accumulating.

But the blenders are excellent for making raw vegetable purées or juices and the combinations you can use are as infinite as the variety of fruits, vegetables and herbs in season during summer.

We give only the basic ingredients in the three following recipes. Amounts to be adjusted to taste and how many you're feeding.

SIMPLE TOMATO BLEND

Ripe tomatoes
Onions
Basil, fresh
Small amount of brown sugar
Salt, freshly ground black pepper

SPICY TOMATO BLEND

Tomatoes
Onion
Green pepper
Basil, fresh
Marjoram, fresh
Thyme, fresh
Garlic
Salt, freshly ground black pepper

BASIC VEGETABLE BLEND

Celery
Tomatoes
Onions
Carrots
Fresh thyme
Worcester sauce
Salt, freshly ground black pepper

If you don't have a blender do try and get a Mouli—a larger version of the popular Baby Mouli—which has three sieve-type discs for coarse, medium or fine mashing. Then any left-over vegetables can be put through the Mouli, thinned with some yoghurt and a little of the cooking water, cooled in the fridge and served garnished with a selection of chopped fresh herbs and a little grated onion.

Below are some recipes that can be made for the warm summer days without any expensive gadgets. If you don't have a Mouli or a blender, just sieve the cooked vegetables, using the back of a wooden spoon to force the mixture through.

RUSSIAN-STYLE BEET SOUP

Cut small beets into cubes, cover with water and cook until tender. Add a dash of vinegar and a good pinch of brown sugar, some salt and about one cup of sour cream (yoghurt will do if you don't have sour cream). Chill and serve with dark bread and a crisp green salad on the side.

BORSCHT—JEWISH-STYLE BEETROOT SOUP

3 large onions
6 medium beetroots
¼ vegetable oil or rendered Chicken Fat (pp. 45-6)
½ cup cooked, stoned prunes
2 Tbs. brown sugar
2-3 pts. water or potato stock
Juice of a lemon or a dash of vinegar
Salt to taste

Lightly brown sliced onions in oil or fat; pour on water or stock and add cubed beets. Let cook until tender. Add lemon juice (or vinegar), prunes, sugar and salt. Put through Mouli and serve either hot or cold with yoghurt or sour cream.

COOL CUCUMBER SOUP

Finely chop two cucumbers. Simmer gently with a medium-sized onion and the following:

Salt to taste
Freshly-ground black pepper
Good pinch of finely ground rosemary
About 1 Tbs. of finely chopped fresh marjoram (or a pinch of it dried)

Take off the fire and stir in four tablespoons of flour; whisk in two cups of water (or some left-over mint tea if you have it). Return to fire and cook a few minutes to thicken.

Mouli the mixture, add a quarter-cup yoghurt and some chopped parsley. Cool and serve.

SIMPLE CUCUMBER SOUP

Grate two large cucumbers and one large onion. Add salt, freshly ground black pepper, and some finely chopped mint and sorrel leaves. Add this mixture to two to three cups of yoghurt thinned with a little iced water. This is an extremely refreshing soup.

DILLWEED SOUP

Don't try to substitute dill seeds for the dillweed—it just won't work. And I'm afraid the dried dillweed is just not as satisfactory as the fresh dill. Which means that unless you grow your own dill you won't be able to make this soup—which is a pity, because it is really excellent, hot or cold.

Make some thick potato stock by cubing two large potatoes and cooking in a heavy pot in which a small sliced onion has been sautéd in some butter. Add enough water to just cover. When the potato is cooked, mash or put through Mouli. The stock should be the consistency of thick pea soup.

To this stock add two beaten eggs mixed with one cup of yoghurt and half a cup of chopped dillweed, salt and pepper to taste. Heat, stirring constantly, but do not let it boil. This soup can be served hot but is best cold.

SUBSTANTIAL SUMMER VEGETABLE SOUP

1 lb. tic (or other) dried beans
1 lb. fresh runner beans
1 bunch celery (tops and all)
4-5 carrots
1 Tbs. chopped parsley

Good pinch each of:
marjoram
basil
thyme
4-5 ripe tomatoes, skinned

Soak tic beans overnight and cook slowly until almost done. Add the runner beans, sliced, diced celery, sliced carrots, herbs and salt to taste, with water to cover.

Be careful not to overcook; when done, add parsley and the ripe tomatoes. Let simmer (but not boil) for about five minutes. Chill and serve during hot weather, when cooking is the last thing you want to do. A large pot of this soup will keep very well in the fridge for a few days.

FRUIT SOUP

1 cup each of stoned plums and cherries, and strawberries
6 cups water (or 5 cups water and 1 cup red wine)
¼ cup brown sugar
Pinch of salt
Juices of half a lemon (or chopped lemon balm)
2 Tbs. cornflour
Chopped fresh mint

Combine fruit, water, sugar, salt and cinnamon in saucepan and cook over low heat for fifteen minutes or until fruit is soft enough to put through Mouli. Mix cornflour with a little water to a smooth paste, then add to fruit mixture. Cook until thickened (and then add the wine, if you're using some, stirring well). Add mint and let cool.

If you're using wine, serve as it is; without the wine this soup is delicious served with yoghurt or sour cream.

MAIN COURSES

Artichokes

Globe artichokes are becoming more popular—not only at the greengrocers but in our gardens. They are handsome plants with their silvery green leaves, looking a bit like an ornamental thistle, and they grow well up north as well as in the south of England.

ARTICHOKES WITH LEMON BUTTER

To cook artichokes wash them and cut off the stem, trimming the leaves of their pointed tops. Place in rapidly boiling water to which a little salt, some olive oil (about one teaspoon per pint of water), and (if desired) a dash of tabasco sauce has been added. Cook for about forty-five minutes or until a leaf will slip off easily. Turn upside down in a saucer to drain. Can be served cold (p. 98) or hot.

Prepare the following lemon butter: melt a quantity

of butter gently, add some lemon juice and finely chopped parsley, salt, freshly ground black pepper. If you are lucky enough to be growing lemon balm, chop this into the butter instead of using lemon juice.

To eat artichokes, just pull of individual leaves and dip the tender part into your sauce, and eat, discarding the upper, tougher part. When all the leaves are gone scrape fuzz off the core, slice and eat with the sauce.

Artichokes cooked simply, as above, are excellent if followed by any one of the mushroom dishes at the end of this section.

STEWED ARTICHOKES, GREEK STYLE

Prepare four artichokes for cooking as above, but rub with some lemon juice and place in well-salted water to keep them from turning black whilst you prepare the following:

2 cups (approx.) shelled broad beans
2 carrots
½ cup spring onions
2 onions, sliced
4 large potatoes
1 Tbs. flour
½ cup chopped fresh dill-weed or 1 full Tbs. dried dill
Salt and freshly ground black pepper
About ½ cup or more olive oil

Put olive oil in good-sized fireproof casserole and sauté onions in it. Cut the carrots, peel the potatoes if you wish (remembering then to save the skins for soup stock) and cube. Add carrots, broad beans, spring onions, potatoes and some salt to the olive oil and onions, and cook until potatoes start to turn a golden crisp colour. Add flour and dill and stir well.

Take off the heat now and arrange the artichokes in the casserole, with their pointed tops upwards and the vegetables tucked in between them. Squeeze some lemon juice onto them, sprinkle with the rest of the salt and the pepper and add just enough hot water to cover the vegetables. Cover the casserole and bake in medium oven (350°F) for about an hour.

STUFFED ARTICHOKES, ITALIAN STYLE

4 large or 6 medium artichokes
1 cup breadcrumbs
2 Tbs. grated Goats' Cheese (pp. 216-19)
2 garlic cloves, crushed
2 Tbs. chopped parsley
6 Tbs. (approx.) olive oil
Salt and freshly ground black pepper

Wash artichokes; cut off stems, remove tough outer leaves and cut off half-inch tips of the artichokes. Tap on table to spread open and shake out all the water.

Thoroughly mix the breadcrumbs, grated cheese, garlic, parsley, salt and pepper. Divide mixture into four (or six) parts and carefully place one portion between the leaves of each artichoke. Then close the artichoke up and place upright in a saucepan. They should fit snugly so that they will not open and spill their contents. Pour about one tablespoon of olive oil on each artichoke and put remaining oil in saucepan. Add one cup of water and cover tightly. Cook slowly over a medium heat for about thirty to forty-five minutes—test by pulling a leaf; if it comes out easily the artichokes are done. Add more water during the cooking if necessary.

This is delicious served with a groats or wheat dish which has been mixed with some basil and thyme.

GREEN BEANS AND TOMATO

This is a very simple dish we used to cook when we lived in southern France—simple but delicious. And it goes very well with a seasoned groat or wheat dish, garnished with freshly chopped basil.

Top and tail runner beans and break into boiling salted water. Cook for ten minutes or so while you heat a small quantity of olive oil in a heavy skillet and sauté a sliced onion and three or four skinned and chopped tomatoes. When this cooks down add some minced garlic and the drained beans. Cook for a further five to ten minutes and serve with the groats or wheat and fresh basil.

SCALLOPED BEANS WITH EGG

2 cups cooked green beans (runner, French or broad)
½ cup grated cheese
3 hard-boiled eggs, sliced
½ pt. White Sauce (p. 199)
About ¼ cup breadcrumbs
Chopped parsley and dill-weed

Grease ovenproof dish; place in a layer of beans, then a layer of egg, alternating until all are used. Pour over white sauce topped with breadcrumbs and grated cheese. Bake in moderate oven (350°F) for fifteen to twenty minutes. Garnish with the parsley and dillweed. Excellent served with new potatoes.

SWEET AND SOUR BEANS

3 cups beans (runner or French)
1 tsp. salt
1 Tbs. flour
2 Tbs. butter
2 Tbs. brown sugar
2 Tbs. vinegar
Salt, freshly ground black pepper
Grated ginger root

Top and tail and break beans into rapidly boiling salted water; cook until done (about twenty minutes), drain and reserve a cup of the bean water for the sauce.

Melt butter in saucepan, add flour and mix thoroughly. Add bean water, stirring constantly, and the rest of the ingredients. Cook gently until thickened, adding more water as needed; finally add the cooked beans and serve over groats.

HARVARD BEETROOT

2 cups cooked, diced beetroot
2 Tbs. brown sugar
2 Tbs. butter
1 Tbs. flour
Pinch of salt
¼ cup vinegar
¼ cup water from cooking beetroot

Set the cooked beetroot aside, covering with the vinegar and water, overnight. Drain, setting aside liquid. Melt butter in saucepan; add flour, stirring well; add sugar, salt, and the liquid from the beets. Cook sauce until it is clear, stirring constantly. Add beets, heat, and serve with a savoury wheat.

SPICY BEETROOT WITH GROATS

2 cups, cooked, diced beetroot
1 cooking apple, grated
1 grated onion
2 Tbs. brown sugar
1 tsp. cinnamon
1 tsp. allspice
Pinch of salt
2 Tbs. butter
1 cup (approx.) water

Melt butter in saucepan and add all the ingredients. Save the water and, stirring well, cook over a medium heat. Add just enough water to keep mixture from sticking to pan.

Serve over plain groats mixed with a handful of currants.

STUFFED COS LETTUCE

Take twelve good-sized cos leaves and gently steam for a few minutes to soften them enough for rolling.

Place some of the following mixture in each leaf and roll up carefully, tucking in the sides.

- 2 cups cooked wheat
- 1 egg
- 1 grated onion
- 1 Tbs. fresh, finely chopped thyme
- 1 Tbs. finely chopped parsley

Place rolled lettuce leaves in greased ovenproof dish. If they are to be eaten cold, pour over a quarter cup hot, salted water and bake in medium oven (350°F) for fifteen to twenty minutes. Serve chilled with simple French Dressing (p. 197).

If they are to be eaten hot, place in greased ovenproof dish, pour over one cup of Cheese Sauce (p. 200), sprinkle with some grated Cheddar cheese and bake in moderate oven for fifteen to twenty minutes.

CHINESE CABBAGE RIBS

Cut out the ribs from each leaf, reserving the leaves for a salad. Cut the ribs into one-inch slices and sauté in some butter with dillseed, salt and black pepper. Serve with an omelette, new potatoes and a salad (made from the leaves of the cabbage).

FRIED GROAT STEW

Here's another recipe using Chinese cabbage—but the variety of vegetables to use can be as extensive as you wish.

- 2 Tbs. oil
- 8 spring onions, chopped
- 2 large carrots, cut in slivers
- 6 Chinese cabbage ribs
- 3 cups cooked and rinsed groats
- 1 egg, beaten
- 1 tsp. soya sauce
- 2 bay leaves

Heat oil in large, heavy skillet and add spring onions and the bay leaves. Sauté for a few minutes; then add vegetables and cook until they just begin to soften. Add groats, gently tossing mixture so it will not stick; cook for about five minutes. Now sprinkle on the soya sauce and pour over the beaten egg. Let mixture cook just enough to harden the egg, still tossing contents gently so it does not become sticky. The vegetables should still be crunchy when served.

All sorts of vegetables may be added or substituted for those given above. Our family is particularly partial to the addition of about a quarter cucumber, chopped. And the addition of some roasted sesame seeds to this dish just before serving is superb.

COURGETTE PANCAKES

4 medium courgettes	Salt to taste
1 onion	Milk to moisten
1 cup flour	Oil (or butter) for frying

Grate the courgettes and onion into bowl; add salt, flour and enough milk to moisten mixture into pancake batter consistency. Heat oil or butter in skillet; drop mixture by spoonfuls, browning well on both sides.

Pancakes can be eaten warm with cheese or White Sauce (p. 199) or cold, topped with a sandwich spread or a little grated cheese.

COURGETTES AND FIELD MUSHROOMS

When we lived in the south of England, one of our favourite wet August pastimes was to wander through fields looking for mushrooms. Now that we are up north we rely more on the woodland mushrooms, but near our shore is a superb patch of field mushrooms which crop bountifully year after year. If you can go and find your own mushrooms, do. Not only is the taste far superior to that of the cultivated mushroom, but it is one of the most pleasurable ways of providing your own food that we know.

The following recipe is excellent made with field mushrooms but can, of course, also be made with the cultivated ones.

1½ cups courgettes, sliced	¼ cup slivered almonds
2 onions, sliced	1 Tbs. chopped fresh marjoram (or a good pinch of the dried)
1 cup sliced mushrooms (sliced thin)	2 Tbs. butter

Combine the onions, courgettes, mushrooms and marjoram. Placed in a skillet in which the butter has been melted, with some salt and a little water if necessary. Cook covered for about fifteen minutes, no longer. Meanwhile, brown the almonds in a little butter. Combine with the courgettes and mushrooms, tossing lightly. Serve on toast, with a green salad.

CHICKEN WITH CUCUMBER

- 1 medium chicken, jointed
- 1 large cucumber
- 1 cup chopped onions
- 3 garlic cloves, minced
- ½ tsp. cardamon, ground
- ½tsp. cinnamon
- Pinch ground cloves
- Pinch mace
- 2 tsp. salt
- 2 Tbs. oil
- 2 cups chicken (or vegetable) broth
- ½ cup (approx.) dessicated coconut for garnish

Wash and dry chicken, and rub with a little salt. Slice cucumber lengthwise into four, then chop each length into half-inch pieces. Set aside in some cold water (preferably in fridge). Combine the chopped onions, garlic and seasonings, mixing very well. Heat oil in deep, heavy skillet and brown the seasoning mixture, then place in the chicken, turning each piece over to coat in the mixture. Add the broth, cover and cook over a medium heat for about an hour, or until done. Add cucumbers, drained, and cook just long enough to heat them (about three to four minutes). Arrange on platter of cooked groats and garnish with dessicated coconut.

FISH AND SEAFOOD

Summer is the season for cheap fish, especially mackerel and, if you're feeling like splurging a little, seafood. It is important to remember that a little seafood will go a long, long way. Some of the recipes below are a bit extravagant, others can be altered to suit your purse, still others are downright economical.

BAKED MACKEREL

6 mackerel, split and boned
2 garlic cloves, crushed
2 tsp. salt
½ tsp. freshly ground black pepper

Mix together the garlic, salt and pepper and rub with your finger tips into the fish. Place the fish in a buttered ovenproof dish and bake for fifteen minutes in a medium oven (350°F). Meanwhile, mix together the following:

½ cup melted butter
4 Tbs. soya sauce
3 Tbs. lemon juice
Pinch of ground chili peppers

Pour half the mixture over the fish and bake for an additional fifteen minutes. Turn fish over and pour remaining mixture over it; return to oven and bake for another ten minutes. Serve with plain cooked wheat garnished with minced parsley.

CURRIED MACKEREL

4 mackerel, filleted
2 cups chopped spring onions
2 cloves garlic, crushed
1 Tsp. grated ginger root or powdered ginger
½ tsp. ground chili peppers
1 tsp. tumeric
2 tsp. salt
½ cup cooked shrimps (optional)
4 Tbs. oil
2 cups green beans, topped, tailed and cut into 1-inch pieces
2 cups water
Lemon Juice
¼ cup currants

Of course, curried mackerel can be made with bought curry powder but we find the above is much better. The spices can be varied (i.e., try adding coriander, cummin and black pepper), but the above has a distinctive taste.

Mix into a paste the garlic, ginger, chili peppers, tumeric, salt and the shrimps. Add the spring onions. Heat oil in heavy skillet and sauté this mixture for a few minutes. Stir in beans and sauté a further few minutes—just long enough for the beans to start to turn bright green. Add water, lemon juice and currants and cook over low heat for five minutes. Place fish gently into the sauce, cover and cook for twenty minutes or so. Serve with plain boiled groats.

POACHED MACKEREL

To one part of white wine add three parts water. Place an onion stuck with cloves, a carrot, some celery and parsley into the water and gently heat. Add top-and-tailed mackerel and cook over gentle heat until fish falls from bone. Strain, keeping liquid, separating fish from bones. Keep fish warm. Make a sauce *béchamel* from some of the liquid. Place fish on cooked groats, pour over the sauce, garnish with some minced parsley and serve with a green salad.

LOBSTER OREGANO

My first contact with lobster was when I was waitressing during my student days in an Italian restaurant in Boston's North End, and I have always kept a preference for the Italian methods of serving lobster.

- 2 medium lobsters
- 6 Tbs. olive oil
- 2 cloves garlic, chopped
- 1 tsp. dried basil or 1 Tbs. fresh, chopped
- 1 Tbs. chopped parsley
- 1 scant tsp. oregano
- ½ cup breadcrumbs
- Salt, pepper to taste
- 2 Tbs. grated cheese

If you are lucky enough to get fresh, live lobsters prepare the recipe as follows:

Sever the spinal cord by inserting a very sharp knife between the body and tail of the lobster; place on back, split the lobster from end to end and spread open. The pinky and green bits *are* edible, but not so the small sac just behind the head which *must* be removed. Crack the large claws.

Place the lobsters in an ovenproof dish, cut-side up;

add about ½ cup water to the pan.

Mix the remaining ingredients (but not the oil) thoroughly and sprinkle over the lobster. Pour over the oil.

Bake in a medium–hot (375°F) oven for about twenty-five minutes or until the lobster meat is tender. Serve hot with buttered pasta and an Onion Salad (p. 100).

If you can only get cooked lobster, prepare as follows:

In deep skillet heat the oil and sauté the garlic, basil, parsley, oregano, salt, pepper and breadcrumbs gently for one minute. Add lobster, tossing gently to coat in the herb mixture. Serve over pasta, sprinkled with the grated cheese.

LOBSTER WITH WHITE WINE (MARINARA)

- 1½ cups cooked lobster
- 4 Tbs. olive oil
- 2-3 cloves garlic, chopped
- ½ cup dry White Wine (pp. 221-3)
- 1 Tbs. chopped parsley
- 4-6 tomatoes, skinned and roughly chopped
- 1 onion, sliced
- Salt and pepper to taste

Brown garlic and onion in saucepan with olive oil; add lobster, salt and pepper and cook for a few minutes to heat through; add tomatoes and cook over medium heat for ten minutes. Add parsley and white wine and just bring up to simmering point. Serve with Broad Pasta (pp. 205-6) and a green salad–spinach is excellent, as it is with Lobster Oregano, above.

JAPANESE BROILED LOBSTER

One last lobster recipe–this from Japan, or so a friend of ours insists. Originally it is made with saké, but dry sherry works well in its place. It's a bit extravagant, but good.

- 4 cups cooked lobster
- 1½ cups (or about 3 bottles) soya sauce
- ½ cup dry sherry
- Dash or so of tabasco sauce
- 3 Tbs. butter, melted

Combine the soya sauce, tabasco and sherry and marinate the cooked lobster in this mixture for a couple of hours. Drain lobster, place in ovenproof dish, baste with butter and bake for ten to fifteen minutes, basting with the marinade frequently.

Serve with groats sautéd with onion and bean sprouts.

The left-over marinade can be used in salad dressings, or poured over groats or wheat before serving with an omelette.

Don't try to use the marinade on the groats that you serve with the lobster as this would make the soya taste a bit too much of a good thing.

CHINESE SHRIMP AND PEAS

- 2 cups cooked shrimp
- 2 Tbs. oil
- 1 tsp. grated ginger root
- 1 clove garlic, minced
- 4-6 chopped spring onions
- 1 cup fresh, shelled peas
- 1 tsp. salt
- 1 tsp. soya sauce
- 1 rounded Tbs. cornflour
- 1 cup chicken broth

Sauté peas, spring onions, garlic, ginger and a sprinkle of the salt for a few minutes (long enough for peas to turn bright green), add shrimp, tossing lightly to coat, and cook a further two to three minutes.

In a separate saucepan mix a little of the chicken broth to the cornflour to form a smooth paste, add rest of the broth, salt, and soya sauce. Cook until thickened; add to the shrimp and peas. Serve immediately with wheat.

SHRIMP OR CRAB FOO YUNG

- ½ cup chopped field mushrooms
- 1 cup cooked shrimp or crab
- 1 cup sliced onions or spring onions
- ½ cup chopped celery tops
- 5 eggs
- 2 tsp. soya sauce
- Dash of tabasco
- Dash of salt
- 4 Tbs. oil

Whisk eggs; blend in all the ingredients except oil. Heat the oil in heavy skillet and drop large spoonfuls of the mixture into it. Brown on both sides and keep hot in oven whilst preparing the following sauce:

1 rounded Tbs. cornflour
2 Tbs. soya sauce
Pinch of sugar
1 cup chicken broth

Combine in usual manner and heat, stirring constantly, until thickened. Pour it over the Foo Yung and serve with plain groats.

SUBSTANTIAL SHRIMP AND VEGETABLES

1 cup cooked shrimp
1 cup sliced onions or spring onions
1 cup celery, tops included, chopped
1 green pepper, sliced
1 cup field mushrooms, sliced
1 cup bean sprouts (optional)
3 Tbs. soya sauce
2 Tbs. dry sherry or white wine
1 tsp. grated ginger root
4 Tbs. oil
1 rounded tsp. cornflour
½ cup chicken broth

Marinade the shrimp, soya sauce and sherry or wine for an hour or so.

Now, in order to ensure that all vegetables are not overcooked, it is best to follow the directions carefully.

Heat half the oil in a skillet and sauté the onions, celery, green peppers and mushrooms for about five minutes. Remove from skillet, and add remaining oil in same skillet and sauté the drained shrimp for about three minutes. Return sautéd vegetables, and add the bean sprouts and the cornflour mixed with the chicken broth. Cook just long enough to thicken, stirring constantly—about five minutes. Excellent served over wheat or groats.

Chicken and other vegetables than those listed can be added to this very tasty Chinese-style dish.

SHRIMP CURRY DELUXE

2 cups cooked shrimp (or chicken and shrimp)
2 onions, thinly sliced
1 cooking apple, chopped
¼ cup butter or chicken fat
¼ cup flour
1 tsp. salt
Freshly-ground black pepper
2 tsp. curry powder
1 tsp. coriander seeds
1 tsp. mustard seeds
2 scant cups chicken broth

Sauté fat, coriander and mustard seeds, curry powder and onions together, stirring constantly. Carefully blend in the flour, salt and pepper and the broth, stirring all the while. Add the shrimp (and/or chicken) and the cooking apple; heat and serve over wheat or groats with the following condiments set out in little bowls:

chopped hard-boiled egg
dessicated coconut
chopped salted nuts
chutney
chopped tomatoes garnished with chopped spring onions

This makes a very festive curry, and a beautiful looking meal to tuck into. If the shrimp is too extravagant, use only chicken, with perhaps a bit of chopped ham. You can vary the ingredients according to your purse and mood.

CREOLE SHRIMP WITH NOODLES

1 cup cooked shrimp
1 sliced onion
1 sliced green pepper
4-6 tomatoes, skinned and chopped
2 Tbs. butter
1 rounded tsp. flour
1 rounded tsp. brown sugar
1 rounded tsp. dried basil or good quantity fresh basil, chopped, to taste

Melt butter, sauté onion until soft; add tomatoes, green pepper and cook until done: about ten minutes. Add basil, brown sugar, salt and freshly ground black pepper to give this sauce a good, spicy taste. Make a paste from the flour and water, and add to the sauce to thicken it.

Adjust seasonings and add the shrimp. Heat and serve hot over Cooked Noodles (pp. 205-6).

STUFFED BAKED MARROW

Marrow was one of those vegetables which I thought were only grown—or over-grown I should say!—for exhibition. But once being presented with one, I devised the following which turned out so well we now grow marrows outselves to eat it more often.

Cut off a lid (sideways) from the marrow and scoop out the seeds. Fill with the following stuffing (or any variation of):

fine chopped onion
grated carrot
1 cup of cooked beans—tic beans are fine
Good quantity chopped dillweed (dill seeds can be substituted)
Salt, black pepper
Garlic, minced

Bind the whole mixture together with beaten egg and fill the marrow to just the top, replacing the lid and tying down. Bake in a fairly hot oven for about one hour or until the sides are crackly. Serve with a side dish of wheat and a green salad.

MARROW FLOWERS IN BATTER

If it is a hot summer and you have a profusion of marrow flowers, try using them in a Tempura Dip (p. 42). They have a very delicate flavour.

I first came across this recipe when living in a remote village in Turkey. One day a woman, leading a donkey laden with deep baskets of the dark golden flowers slung on either side of its back, appeared at my doorway. She told me how to prepare the batter, and fry the flowers to a golden brown. If you don't want to make them like the tempura, then simply beat up an egg, add a bit of flour and some salt, and dip the flowers, holding them by their stalk, into the egg, and then pop them into a frying pan in which butter is just sizzling. Eat them while hot and crisp with yoghurt on the side.

MUSHROOMS AND NOODLES

1 lb. field mushrooms
2 green peppers
1 onion, sliced
½ cup of butter

Melt the butter and sauté the onion; reduce heat to low and add sliced green peppers and mushrooms. While this is cooking, prepare the sauce:

1 tsp. dried mustard
1 Tbs. of Worcester sauce
1 bay leaf
1 sprig of rosemary
1 cup of red wine
Salt, black pepper to taste

Combine the Worcester sauce and the dried mustard. Add the wine, bay leaf, sprig of rosemary, salt and black pepper. Now add this to the onions, mushrooms and peppers, letting it simmer gently for about thirty minutes. Serve over Noodles (pp. 205-6), after removing bay leaf and sprig of rosemary.

MUSHROOMS AND PEAS OVER WHEAT

1 lb. mushrooms, sliced
2 cups shelled peas
1 onion, sliced
4 Tbs. butter
2 bay leaves
1 tsp. crushed thyme
1 cup vegetable broth
1 cup red wine
2 Tbs. tomato paste
1 Tbs. chopped parsley
Salt and black pepper to taste

Sauté onions in butter with bay leaves, thyme and a little salt; add mushrooms and shelled peas and toss. When the peas begin to soften and brighten in colour, add the broth, wine, tomato paste and the parsley. Add rest of salt and pepper and let all simmer for about thirty minutes by which time the liquid should have been reduced to a thick sauce. Remove bay leaves and serve over wheat.

STUFFED GREEN PEPPERS, HOT

8 firm green peppers, lids cut from the tops and seeds scooped out
½ lb. minced meat (beef, mutton, lamb)
1 cup pre-cooked wheat
1 tomato, skinned and diced
2 cloves garlic, crushed
1 tsp. oregano
1 tsp. basil
Salt, black pepper

Mix all the ingredients except the peppers; stuff some of the mixture into each of the peppers. Replace the tops and arrange the peppers in a greased pot (if you are going to cook them on top of the stove) or in a greased casserole (if you are going to bake them). If in a pot, gently simmer, adding a little liquid to them, closely covered, for about thirty minutes. If in the oven, add a little water, cover, and bake in a medium oven for forty-five minutes.

Serve with wheat, making a sauce for the peppers if desired as follows: add enough cornflour (about one tablespoon to a cup) to the cooking water, with a little tomato sauce and some basil, salt and pepper, to thicken, cooking for a few minutes. A little chopped parsley can be added for colour.

STUFFED GREEN PEPPERS, COLD

6 green peppers, lidded and cleaned as above
2 cups pre-cooked wheat
1 egg
Good bunch of chopped fresh dill or 2 Tbs. dried dillweed
4 tomatoes, skinned and cubed
2 Tbs. chopped parsley
2 Tbs. olive oil
1 medium onion, grated
Salt, pepper

Combine the wheat, seasonings and the tomato. Mix well. Add beaten egg, olive oil and mix thoroughly. Divide the mixture into the peppers and arrange them in a greased pot, adding some water. Closely cover and cook over a medium heat for about thirty minutes, or in an oven as above. Chill and serve with seasoned groats, or in combination with other salads.

NEW POTATOES

There is something really lovely about digging your first potatoes, and then eating them. Nothing tastes quite as good as the season's first potatoes.

Melt a little butter in a heavy saucepan and lightly brown a sliced onion. Add potatoes and either some bay leaves or a sprig of fresh mint, water to just cover and cook for about twenty minutes—don't let the potatoes get mushy. Drain (but save for soups) the water, sprinkle some oatmeal over the potatoes, toss them about to cover, let cook for four to five minutes and serve. This is delicious served with an omelette (below) and a green salad.

SWEET AND SOUR RABBIT

The following two rabbit recipes Tony knew from Australia. If you can bag your own, great. Otherwise, try your local butcher.

1½ lb. (approx.) cut rabbit
2 Tbs. oil
¼ cup brown sugar
2 Tbs. cornflour
¼ cup vinegar
1 cup fruit juice
1 Tbs. soya sauce
2 green peppers, sliced
½ cup parsley, chopped
½ cup spring onion, chopped
½ lb. stoned plums or gooseberries

Have the rabbit cut into smallish pieces and brown in hot oil. Add a little water and cook slowly, stirring occasionally, until tender. Mix brown sugar, cornflour, vinegar, fruit juice and soya sauce. Cook together until it thickens, stirring constantly. Pour over the rabbit and simmer for a few minutes. Now add plums or gooseberries, onion, green peppers and parsley. Simmer together for five to ten minutes and serve over groats.

RABBIT AND MUSHROOM CASSEROLE

- 1 rabbit, cleaned and jointed
- ½ lb. field mushrooms
- 1 onion, sliced
- 1 Tbs. each of parsley, thyme marjoram
- 2 Tbs. butter
- Well seasoned flour for drenching
- 1 cup white wine
- 1 Tbs. flour

Soak the rabbit overnight in well-salted water. Dry the pieces and roll well in well-seasoned flour. Melt butter and gently brown the meat; remove and place in greased casserole. Cook the mushrooms and onions in what butter remains until they are soft. Blend in the flour, then stir in the wine carefully, and cook until it thickens. Add the herbs and pour over the rabbit. Cover with greaseproof paper or just buttered heavy brown paper, place lid on casserole and cook in medium oven for about one-and-a-half to two hours.

Serve with boiled potatoes and parsley.

SPINACH PANCAKES

No matter how hard we try to organize the garden, there always comes a time when we have a glut of greens. So what to do with them if I've already put enough by, by way of relishes and pickles for the winter? Then sudden inspiration. In Italy and southern France I remembered seeing drying racks of green spaghetti in small pasta shops. And, if spaghetti, why not pancakes?

- 3 cups cooked spinach or other greens, including thinnings, carrot tops, etc.
- 2 eggs, well beaten
- ¼ cup vegetable oil
- 1 cup milk, soured with a little vinegar
- ½ cup oatmeal
- 1½ cups flour
- Salt, black pepper
- 1 grated onion
- 2 cloves garlic, minced
- Scant teaspoon ground cummin (optional)

Mix together all the dry ingredients; combine the milk,

a little of the oil and the beaten eggs. Now combine this mixture with the greens and the grated onion. Heat some oil in a heavy skillet; drop mixture in by generous spoonfuls. Brown on both sides and serve with Cheese Sauce (p. 200), Mushroom Sauce (p. 200), yoghurt or sour cream.

SPINACH AND YOUNG TURNIPS

4 Tbs. butter
2 onions, finely chopped
2 tsp. coriander seeds
Pinch each of ground
  tumeric
  cayenne pepper
1 tsp. salt
½ cup yoghurt

2 lbs. spinach (or other greens), coarsely chopped
6-8 young turnips, sliced thin
2 cloves garlic, crushed or minced
1 tomato, skinned and diced

Heat the butter and add the coriander seeds. When they begin to pop, add the onion and sauté until soft. Add rest of the spices, salt and the yoghurt and cook for a further five minutes, stirring constantly so that yoghurt will not stick to the pan.

Add half the spinach to the spice mixture along with the turnips, garlic and tomato. Cook, covered for a few minutes and then add the rest of the spinach and about half a cup of water. Cook for a further fifteen to twenty minutes or until the turnips are tender. Serve with wheat or groats.

SUMMER OMELETTE

Most of the egg recipes are in the Spring chapter, for that is when eggs are most plentiful. But the following is a special summer omelette, as it calls for fresh mint.

For every two eggs you use, add one tablespoon of salty Goat's Cheese (pp. 216-7), grated or crumbled. (It's not always easy to grate this cheese as it naturally tends to crumble. In Turkey, in the old food markets, very salty, dry, crumbled goat's cheese is sold exclusively for serving with pastas.) Beat the eggs and the cheese together, add as much finely chopped mint and grated pepper as you wish, and cook in hot butter in a heavy skillet. Delicious served with a tossed green salad as a light supper or lunch.

CURRIED SUMMER VEGETABLE DISH

This is an extremely colourful and flavourful dish. If possible, make it truly festive by serving with side dishes of dessicated coconut and salted nuts.

- 2 cups shelled broad beans
- 1 green pepper, sliced
- 1 onion, sliced
- 3-4 tomatoes, skinned and diced
- 1 large ear of sweet corn, boiled
- 2 tbs. oil
- 1 tsp. curry powder
- ½tsp. each of
  - mustard seed
  - coriander seed

Heat oil in heavy skillet; add curry, seeds and onions, cooking until the latter are transparent. Add broad beans and sauté for a few minutes. When the beans turn a bright green, add the pepper and tomatoes. Cook for ten minutes then scrape the corn kernels from the cob with a knife. Add these and cook a further five minutes. Serve with boiled groats lightly browned in garlic-flavoured oil.

ROASTED SWEET CORN

Sweet corn does not grow in all parts of Britain; unfortunately is not even available in all parts of Britain. I find this very sad because I love sweet corn which, being plentiful in the North-Eastern States, I always took for granted. So each year I try to grow sweet corn in my window, in my garden, under plastic—anywhere. However, Skye is not the best place to try and grow sweet corn and so the results are variable, to say the least. But in my eagerness to grow, and eat, sweet corn I have even cooked the whole very young ears in a little water, seasoned with butter, salt and pepper, and eaten them whole. They're actually quite good, so if your sweet corn doesn't mature into those lovely fat ears with brown silk cascading down from the tip, as it shows on the packet of seeds, don't despair.

But if they do grow into nice, well-behaved, fat ears, try cooking them the following way. It is absolutely superb. (If you're buying the corn, buy nice firm ears, with all their light green leaves nice and moist and the silk brown. Don't open the ears to peek and check if all the kernels are even, or even there! Trust that they are.)

Make a wood fire somewhere on a beach or out in your garden or even in your sitting room grate. When the wood has burned down to glowing red coals, simply place the ears of corn, still enclosed in their leaves, right on the coals, and heap more coals over them. When the leaves look thoroughly charred and black and you can't possibly imagine eating anything that looks so burnt, take out the ears, peel off the leaves and you will find the most tender corn you've ever had. Just sprinkle on some salt, knife on some butter, and enjoy.

SOME SUMMER SPECIALITIES

Trout and salmon must rate, from the point of view of both the ecologist and the gourmet, as *the* specialities of this season. They must, of course, be freshly caught, and if you are fortunate enough to have landed a few, or been handed some, use one of the recipes below.

TROUT

Trout is best split, cooked in plenty of butter, and served sprinkled with a little salt and equal amounts of fresh chopped parsley and dill. New boiled potatoes and a crisp green salad complete this truly simple but elegant dish.

SALMON

Salmon, being a larger fish, is more versatile. And, as it is absolutely delicious smoked, I want first to give directions for curing your own fish. The following is suitable for mackerel, haddock, and any other fish you'd like to try.

CURING AND SMOKING

Scale, slit the fish up the back and clean. Wipe with a damp cloth but do not wash. For every 20 lb. of fish you will need one cup of salt (ordinary cooking salt will do) and one cup of sugar. Some also add 1 oz. of saltpetre but I do not find this necessary at all.

Mix the sugar and salt together and rub well all over the fish. Lay the fish (one over another if more than one fish) in a stone crock, weighed down with a board and stone on top. They should be well pressed down. Let stand for five days.

Lift fish out and place on clean board to drain; do not wash, simply let them drain for a bit. Then wipe dry, stretch them open and peg open onto a board.

Make a wood fire in your garden, using plenty of green wood once the coals are hot. Stack the fish around the fire and place a wooden barrel over the fish and fire. The fish should stay in this improvised smokehouse for a further five days, after which time take them off the board and keep dry in a cool place.

If the fire goes out (which it invariably will do) and you find that the smoke has escaped, simply light another fire. The fire can be quite tiny—it is the smoke that counts.

BAKED WHOLE STUFFED SALMON

Scale and clean fish; sprinkle with salt and pepper and fill with the following stuffing:

½ cup breadcrumbs
½ cup cracker crumbs
1 egg
¼ cup melted butter
1 small chopped onion
1 Tbs. chopped fresh dill-weed
1 Tbs. chopped fresh parsley
1 tsp. salt

Mix all the ingredients well and stuff the fish, sewing up the cavity. Place in a greased pan and place in a hot (400°F) oven, allowing about ten to twelve minutes per pound of fish, and basting every ten minutes with some of the escaping juice.

Serve hot, as it is, or with the following cold sauce:

1 cup cream, beaten stiff, to which has been added ¼ lb. finely grated horseradish root

BAKED SLICED SALMON

If a friend has caught a large salmon and given you a few slices, try cooking them this way:

4 slices salmon
2 Tbs. butter
2 tsp. salt
Pinch of black pepper
1 onion, sliced
1 bay leaf
A little fresh, chopped thyme
1 cup single cream

Melt the butter in a baking dish and arrange salmon slices, sprinkled with salt, pepper and the thyme, with the sliced onion and bay leaf. Bake in moderate-hot (375°F) oven for fifteen minutes; pour cream over fish and bake for an additional twenty minutes, basting frequently.

MARINATED SALMON

6 slices salmon
2 large onions, sliced into rounds
3 cups water
2 tsp. salt

Combine the above ingredients in a large saucepan and bring to the boil; simmer gently for twenty-five minutes, then carefully transfer salmon and onion rings to a bowl.

To the fish stock, add:

½ cup lemon juice
½ cup white vinegar
1 rounded tsp. pickling spice
1 bay leaf
4 sprigs dillweed, chopped

Bring this to a boil, cooking for two minutes; pour over

the fish and chill for at least twenty-four hours before serving. It will keep and improve in flavour in the fridge for four days.

SALMON TARTARE

For every 4 lb. of boiled fish, prepare the following tartare:

- 4 hard-boiled eggs
- 1 tsp. mustard powder
- 1 Tbs. olive oil
- ¼ cup Mayonnaise (pp. 198-9)
- 1 Tbs. Ketchup (pp. 152-3)
- 1 Tbs. white wine (or cider) vinegar
- 1 Tbs. chopped parsley
- 1 cup fish stock
- 1 rounded Tbs. each of chopped Pickled
  - Nasturtims (p. 150)
  - Cucumbers (pp. 147-9)
  - Onions (pp. 150-51)

Separate the white from the yolks and chop the whites fine, putting aside with the other chopped vegetables. Rub the yolks smooth with the mustard and the oil, and add the rest of the ingredients, beating well with a wooden spoon, adding the chopped ingredients last. Taste and add salt and pepper.

Place cold fish on crisp lettuce and pour over the tartare or place the tartare in a bowl, and let everyone take as much as they like.

SALADS

Salads, like soups, can be infinitely varied; one is limited only by the vegetables available and the dressings to be used. Or the salads can be simple so as to better off-set a particularly intriguing main dish. But whatever the occasion, salads are always in demand, especially in the summer.

BASIC GREEN SALAD

For an excellent tossed green salad, use crisp lettuces, Chinese cabbage leaves, young spinach and dandelion, curly endive with a few leaves of young sorrel and borage or comfrey, chopped fairly fine. Cress, fennel and celery tops can also be used.

If you want something with a bit more body to it, add hard-boiled, sliced eggs, cold fish or meat, small hunks of cheese, radishes, spring onions, sticks of carrot, raw young mushrooms, young cubed turnips, fresh shelled beans or peas, sliced celery stalks, sliced green peppers, sunflower or pumpkin seeds, bean sprouts or nuts. But if you are making a full-bodied salad, then it is important to remember that the leafy greens should comprise about half of the salad and the whole be tossed in a simple vinaigrette dressing.

Or, if you're using only the greens, you can make a delicious dressing in your salad bowl. Simply rub the bowl with a clove of garlic; discard clove, and place greens which have been washed in cold water and tossed dry, in the bowl. Pour over a little olive oil; toss to coat the greens. Now sprinkle on some Wine Vinegar (p. 196), salt and freshly ground black pepper. Toss again and serve.

It's not difficult to make a good salad dressing, as the recipes in the last chapter (pp. 196-9) show. And a good salad makes such a difference to a meal.

ARTICHOKES WITH VINAIGRETTE

Prepare artichokes, choosing small ones so each person can have one, as directed on p. 73. Chill.

Place artichokes, stem-side down, on small plates. Pour a little vinaigrette dressing over each and serve, passing around a small bowl of dressing for dipping the leaves.

Alternatively, the artichokes can be split in half lengthwise, the fuzzy core cut out, and the artichokes placed on individual plates, the vinaigrette being poured into the hollow.

CASSEROLE VEGETABLE SALAD

Choose a glass casserole so that you can see the layers of vegetables.

Place into the dish alternate layers of sliced tomatoes, sliced cucumbers, thin-sliced onion rings and sliced green peppers. Between each layer place a generous sprinkling of freshly chopped basil leaves, salt and pepper. Pour over this a dressing of about three-quarters of a cup of vinaigrette dressing, to which some dry mustard has been added. Cover tightly and chill overnight to allow the flavours to blend.

CHICKEN SALAD IN BASKETS

With half the recipe for Puff Pastry (pp. 207-8), make the baskets by rolling out the dough thinly, cutting it into rounds and gently pressing these into little cake tins. Prick and bake in hot oven.

Prepare the chicken salad as follows:

- 2 cups cooked diced chicken
- 1 cup celery, chopped
- 2 hard-boiled eggs

Marinade chicken and celery in a simple vinaigrette dressing overnight. Drain off any excess dressing and keep aside, mixing with a little Mayonnaise (pp. 198-9) to form a thick cream-type dressing. Pour this over the chicken and celery, adding the hard-boiled eggs. Fill the puff baskets, and garnish with sprigs of parsley.

CRAB SALAD

- 1 medium crab
- ¼ cucumber, diced
- 2-3 sticks celery, chopped
- 1 small green pepper, diced
- 1 Tbs. chopped parsley
- 8 chopped spring onions
- ½ cup Mayonnaise (pp. 198-9)
- ½ cup Yoghurt (pp.218-9)
- Juice of half a lemon
- Salt, black pepper
- Extra sprigs of parsley (or cress) to garnish

Take meat out of body and claws of crab and mix with all ingredients, except the garnish greens. Toss so everything is coated and place in shallow bowl, around which you put the extra parsley or cress.

CROWDIE SALAD

For every half cup of Crowdie (p. 216) to be used, add one tablespoon of cream, salt, pepper and chopped parsley. Cream and add some chopped nuts and toasted sesame seeds. Form into balls about the size of a walnut and place on crisp lettuce, along with some sliced radishes and chopped spring onion. Pour over a little Mayonnaise (pp. 198-9) thinned with some yoghurt.

CUCUMBERS, TURKISH STYLE

Take cucumbers and cut, lengthwise, into four; now chop into half-inch pieces and drop into salted iced water for about an hour. Meanwhile, take some yoghurt, which should be fairly runny; if yours is thick, thin with a little iced water. Add as much crushed garlic as you like, salt, black pepper and a pinch or so of dried mint. Combine with the drained cucumbers and serve in shallow plates. Delicious served with Pidé (pp. 211-2).

CUCUMBERS, WITH SOUR CREAM

Prepare cucumbers as above, drain and cover with the following dressing:

To each half cup of sour cream add one tablespoon of lemon juice, vinegar, a pinch of sugar and one teaspoon of salt. Mix well, and garnish with thinly sliced onion rings and some chopped parsley. If you have fresh dill-weed, chop up about two tablespoons and use in the dressing. Chill before serving, to blend the flavours.

SIMPLE SPINACH AND ONION SALAD

Thinly slice some onions, separating the rings, and cover with lemon juice, salt, and some olive oil. Set aside to marinade for at least an hour. Pour this over some washed young spinach leaves, toss, and serve.

SIMPLE TOMATO SALAD

Thickly slice some tomatoes and put them into a bowl. Grate a little onion over them, then add some chopped fresh (or dried) basil, dillweed, salt and black pepper. Toss until the tomatoes are evenly coated. Add olive oil and wine vinegar in the proportion of three:one (i.e., three tablesponns of oil to one of vinegar). Toss again and chill well.

SIMPLE RUNNER BEAN SALAD

Top and tail runner beans, break into pieces and drop into well-salted boiling water. Cook until just tender (and still a little crunchy). Drain.

Prepare a dressing by adding to a simple vinaigrette some crushed garlic and one small minced onion. Toss beans in the dressing, and chill well.

SIMPLE TURKISH SALAD

This is not so simple, but more a construction, and should be placed in the centre of your table, allowing everyone to take from it what they choose.

On a large platter arrange crisp lettuce leaves broken into convenient sizes for spearing. Now season this with a sprinkling of salt, pepper, a squeeze of lemon or white vinegar and a little olive oil. Arrange on the lettuce leaves some sliced or crumbled Goat's Cheese (p. 44) sprinkled with oregano and a little olive oil. Arrange in patterns sliced cucumbers and tomatoes, sprinkled with salt and pepper, and some sliced green peppers. Sprinkle with a little more olive oil and vinegar or lemon juice (lemon juice is really best), some more oregano and, if you really feel like going on the town, use dark black olives too.

DESSERTS

Summer is fruit time, especially berries, and so we'll concentrate on these, omitting the more traditional and well-worn recipes.

The first strawberries of the season you will no doubt want to eat chilled, with a sprinkling of icing sugar and some fresh whipped cream. And that's how Tony remembers them from Australia. But in the Eastern States strawberries were generally served as follows:

STRAWBERRY SHORTCAKE

First you must make some biscuits, thus: mix together two cups of self-raising flour, one teaspoon of salt and two tablespoons of sugar; work into this half a cup of butter with a fork, and add about three-quarters of a cup of milk quickly. Do not overmix. Toss onto floured surface, pat and roll to about one-inch thickness. Cut into rounds and bake on greased pan in a hot oven (450° F) for ten to fifteen minutes, or until golden brown.

Split the biscuits and fill with slightly crushed strawberries, sweetened with sugar if desired. Place the other half of the biscuit on top, add a dollop of freshly whipped cream, decorate with whole fresh strawberries, and serve.

STRAWBERRY TORTEN

A very fancy strawberry dessert is this berry torten. A torten is a cake without butter, relying on plenty of eggs for lightness. It also does not have flour, but generally has cracker crumbs, nuts or even bread.

- 8 egg whites, beaten stiff and dry (Keep the egg yolks for mayonnaise or other sauces—or for brushing tops of bread or rolls to be baked.)
- 1 cup icing sugar
- 1 cup almonds, chopped fine or put through grinder
- 1 tsp. vanilla
- 2 lb. fresh strawberries
- Whipping cream

Add sugar gradually to the stiffly beaten egg whites; add flavouring. Lastly the chopped nuts should be folded in. Spread this mixture evenly onto two well-buttered, floured cake tins and bake in a moderate oven (350° F) for twenty-five to thirty minutes.

When cool, place strawberries—cut and sugared if desired—and whipped cream between layers and on the top. Decorate the very top with whole strawberries and a few fresh mint leaves.

STRAWBERRY CHIFFON PIE

This is an excellent recipe for using up bruised fruit. And any other berries can be substituted for the strawberries.

1 baked pie shell
1 Tbs. gelatin
¼ cup cold water
½ cup boiling water
½ cup sugar
Pinch of salt
1 cup strawberries, mashed to pulp
2 egg whites
2 Tbs. sugar (for egg whites)
½ cup whipped cream
Whipped cream for garnish

Soak gelatin in the cold water for five minutes; then combine the boiling water, sugar, strawberry pulp and salt. Add softened gelatin and stir until dissolved. While this cools, beat the egg whites until they are stiff and dry. Gradually beat in the sugar.

Fold whipped cream into the gelatin mixture when the latter has begun to thicken. Now fold in the egg whites and pour the mixture into the baked pie shell. Chill and serve, garnished with whipped cream.

Gooseberries are plentiful too, and easy to grow. In the next section is a recipe for pickling them; once you've done this and have had the traditional gooseberry puddings and pies, try one of the two recipes below.

GOOSEBERRY MERINGUE

1 pie shell
2 cups cooked gooseberries, mashed with sugar to taste
2 eggs, separated
¼ cup icing sugar

Blend beaten egg yolks into the gooseberry pulp once it has cooled. Pour into the pie shell and bake for twenty minutes in a hot oven (375°F).

Meanwhile, whisk egg whites until stiff and dry; gradually mix in icing sugar. Spread on top of pie, return to the oven, which has now been turned off, and bake just until the meringue is brown—about three to five minutes.

GOOSEBERRY ROLL

About 1½ cups cooked gooseberries, mashed with sugar to taste
5 eggs, separated
1 cup sugar
1 cup flour
2 Tbs. lemon juice
Grated rind of one lemon

Put well-mashed gooseberries aside, while you prepare the roll.

Beat egg yolks well, add sugar and beat until thick and foamy. Add lemon juice and grated rind, half the flour and half the egg whites (which have been beaten stiff and dry) alternately, then rest of the whites and flour gradually. Pour batter, not more than a quarter-inch thick, onto well greased pans which have also been lined with greased paper. Bake in a hot oven (375°F) for twelve to fifteen minutes. Turn on sheet of heavy paper or onto a damp cloth. Spread with the gooseberry mixture and roll whilst still warm. Wrap in paper until cool.

FRUIT BOWL SUPERB

When there is so much fresh fruit about, it seems best, no matter how tasty the recipes, to have it fresh and simply—at least some of the time.

Start with some top-and-tailed gooseberries, currants and strawberries, and place these in a bowl; add stoned plums, cherries, and any other available fruit.

Now make a dressing for this with equal parts of honey and wine and pour over the fruit, tossing it well. If it is not sweet enough, add more honey. (It might be necessary to slightly warm the honey to make the dressing.) Place the bowl in a fridge and let it marinate. Before serving, toss again and add some chopped lemon balm leaves. Serve with Pound Cake (p. 106).

I haven't mentioned raspberries yet, although they can be used in many of the above recipes. However, below are two excellent recipes especially for raspberries.

RASPBERRY PUDDING DELUXE

2 cups vanilla custard (As given in recipe for Layered Pudding, p. 62)
3-4 cups fresh raspberries
Sugar to taste
¾ cup whipping cream
2-3 drops of vanilla

Chill the vanilla custard, making sure it is nice and thick. Mash the fresh raspberries and put through a sieve to get rid of the seeds if you wish. Sweeten to taste, and add vanilla. Whip the cream until thick.

Combine the custard and the raspberries, mixing thoroughly. Now fold in the whipped cream gently with a fork, so that the cream does not combine but leaves streaks through the bright pink pudding. Put into individual glasses and chill before serving. Thinly sliced Pound Cake (p. 106) goes well with this dish.

RASPBERRY CREAM

4 cups fresh berries (strawberries can be used instead)
¾ cup sugar (or less)
2 Tbs. gelatin
¼ cup cold water
¼ cup boiling water
½ pt. whipping cream

Wash berries (putting aside a few for decoration). Sugar them and let stand overnight or a few hours, then crush.

Dissolve the gelatin in the cold water for five minutes, add the boiling water and stir until thoroughly dissolved. When cool, add the crushed fruit and its juice and, when this begins to thicken, fold in the stiffly beaten whipped cream. Place in a glass bowl and decorate with the whole berries and some fresh lemon balm and/or mint leaves. Chill for a couple of hours at least.

AMERICAN POUND CAKE

This is an excellent cake for baking during the summer months because it will keep very well, so you can bake these three loaves and keep them in aluminium foil. Sliced thin, it is an excellent accompaniment to summer fruit puddings.

- 1 lb. flour
- 1 lb. butter
- 1 lb. sugar
- 9-10 eggs (which is about 1 lb.)
- 2 Tbs. vanilla; (brandy or sherry flavouring can be substituted with excellent results)

Sift the flour so it is light; cream the butter and gradually add the sugar, until mixture is light and fluffy. Add eggs to the butter and sugar mixture, beating thoroughly after each addition. Finally add the flavouring. Now add the flour gradually, beating to keep the mixture very smooth.

Grease and line three loaf tins with oiled paper; divide mixture evenly among the three tins and bake at 300°F for about an hour or more. Turn out and cool.

Finally, some berry pies which always are a favourite, and delicious served with ice cream.

CHERRY PIE

- 4 cups sour cherries, stoned
- 1½-2 cups sugar
- 2 Tbs. cornflour
- 1 Quick Pie Pastry (p. 207)

Line a flan dish with half the pastry. Mix together the fruit, sugar and cornflour and fill crust. Cover with the rest of the pastry rolled into strips and placed criss-cross on the top. Bake in a hot oven (450°F) for about twenty minutes; then reduce heat and bake for a further ten minutes. If the edges threaten to brown too much, cover with aluminium foil.

GOOSEBERRY PIE

2 cups gooseberries, topped and tailed
Scant cup sugar, spiced with grated ginger and nutmeg and about 1 tsp. cinnamon
Water if necessary
Quick Pie Pastry (p. 207)

Cook the gooseberries and sugar, adding water if necessary, just until the fruit is softened. Line flan dish with half the pastry and fill with the fruit. Cover with the other half, fluting the edges and pricking the top. Bake as for Cherry Pie, above.

RED OR BLACK CURRANT PIE

1 cup ripe currants
1 cup sugar
¼ cup flour
2 eggs, separated
1 Tbs. water
1 flan dish lined with Pie Dough (p. 207)

Wash and top and tail the currants, and combine with the sugar and flour. Beat egg yolks slightly, adding the water, and combine this with the currant mixture. Turn into the lined flan and bake for twenty minutes in a hot oven (375°F). Meanwhile, whisk egg whites, combining them with a little sugar when they are stiff. Spread over hot currant pie and return to the now-turned-off oven for three to five minutes—just long enough for the meringue to brown.

RASPBERRY PIE

4 cups raspberries
¾ (approx.) cup sugar
2 Tbs. plain flour
Juice of half a lemon
Little grated nutmeg
Pie Dough (p. 207)

Mix the fruit with the sugar, flour, lemon and spice. Line a flan dish with half of the pie dough; cover with other half, prick surface, brush with milk and bake in a hot oven (375°F) for about thirty minutes.

PRESERVES, PICKLES, CHUTNEYS

I use the large sweet jars in which to make and store my pickles and relishes. They look good and I like to recycle these very useful jars which, unfortunately, are being replaced by plastic ones.

DILL GREEN BEANS

Take any quantity of green beans, top, tail, and break into pieces. Cook in salted water (two teaspoons of salt to two pints of water) for about five minutes. Drain and pack into layers in a crock, packing in a good quantity of fresh dill (stalk and all), some peppercorns and broken bits of bay leaf between each layer. Top with more dill and tuck some large leaves (dock, cherry, cabbage) over the top. Top up with vinegar, making sure that the beans and leaf are well below the surface—weigh down with a stone or a plate if necessary. Let stand in a warm place (but out of direct sunlight) for about one week. Rinse off any scum that rises to the top and add more vinegar if necessary. In another three to four days the beans should be done and can be put into clean glass jars, topped with fresh vinegar or with brine (one cup salt to five of water). Keep in a cool, dry place.

PICKLED CHERRIES

Stone two pounds of sour cherries and place in crock; cover with vinegar and let stand for twenty-four hours, stirring a few times. Drain vinegar. Measure same amount of sugar as cherries and place in crock in layers, ending with sugar. Stir each day until sugar is dissolved. In three days the cherries can be packed in clean jars and sealed. This is a nice accompaniment to curries.

Gooseberries can be treated the same way.

SUMMER DILL PICKLED CUCUMBERS

If you use gherkins, keep them whole; if the long ridge cucumbers, cut them lengthwise into quarters. Soak the cucumbers overnight in cold water. Drain and dry; place in large crock in layers with a good quantity of black peppercorns, broken bay leaves, slivered garlic cloves and lots of fresh dill between the cucumbers. Pour over water (to every four pints, add half a cup of salt), tuck large leaves over top and weigh down with stone or plate. Leave to ferment for a week, skimming off any scum that arises.

After a week, take out cucumbers, place in clean jars with some fresh dill and pour over spiced vinegar to cover. Keep in cool place.

There are more recipes for preserving cucumber in the Autumn chapter.

PICKLED EGGS

12 hard-boiled, shelled, eggs
1 pt. vinegar spiced with
 1 tsp. black peppercorns
 1 tsp. mace
 Some bruised ginger root
½ pt. water salted with
 2 tsp. salt

Place eggs in crock; pour over the spiced vinegar and water which has been previously boiled together. When cold, cover and store in cool place. Be sure that the eggs are below the surface of the liquid.

SPICED GOOSEBERRIES

2 lb. very green, very firm gooseberries
1½ cups brown sugar
½ pt. vinegar
1 Tbs. cinnamon
1 tsp. whole cloves
1 tsp. allspice

Wash, top and tail fruit.

Bring vinegar, sugar and spices to the boil; add the

berries and simmer for twenty minutes. Pack berries into clean jars, topping with the vinegar, seal and store in cool place. Good as a side dish with oriental-style meals.

HERBAL TEAS

In our garden we try to grow herbs which are difficult to get or which I want to dry myself for teas. At the moment we have the following growing: fennel, dill, coriander, sage, thyme, marjoram, basil, balm, caraway, tarragon, rosemary, bay, camomile, hyssop and winter savory. I use all of these, except the dill, coriander, basil and caraway, for teas.

To add to these, we also collect mint, wild roses, rose hips, honeysuckle, elder flowers, ling (heather), gorse leaf buds (which have a delicate coconut flavour), cowberry leaves, yarrow and meadowsweet.

When picking your herbs, try to pick in the morning after the dew has dried. Never pick wet. Pick only the healthiest of plants, leaving about one-third to regenerate itself for the rest of the season or the following year.

For large plants such as mints, sage, yarrow or meadowsweet, tie the stems loosely together and hang upside down to dry in a warm place. I hang ours from beams in our kitchen. Small flowers should be dried in a paper bag and hung. After drying, separate and gather the useful from the unwanted parts, and store in air tight containers.

Make herbal teas as you would ordinary tea—in a hot teapot to which is added the tea and then the freshly boiled water. But herbal teas look best (and we think taste better!) served in glasses rather than china cups. In fact, it is lovely to float some rose petals in the glasses.

The mixing of herbal teas is, I think, purely an individual matter. However, below are a few mixtures to give you some idea of what can be combined with what.

BREAKFAST TEA

To one handful of dried blackcurrant leaves, add two tablespoons of dried ling flowers, some wild rose petals, a pinch of cowberry leaves and some dried grated orange peel. Shake and store.

Or take a good handful of lemon verbena or lemon balm, add some crushed cinnamon bark, some crushed cloves and some grated dried orange peel.

MEALTIME TEAS

Take equal amounts of mint, yarrow, marjoram and some lemon balm. Or, equal amounts of meadowsweet, fennel with a touch of sage.

SAVOURY PICK-ME-UP TEAS

Using marjoram as a base, add some crushed cummin seed, a little ginger root and some lemon balm.

Or, use equal amounts of comfrey, strawberry leaves and blackberry leaves. To this add some mint, elder flowers and sage.

Chapter Four
Autumn

SOUPS

In the preceding chapter there are two recipes for beet soup which can be served either hot or cold though are, we feel, best cool. I'll begin this section with another beet soup, but this one made with Boletus mushrooms—or cultivated mushrooms, but they are definitely not as good.

Boletus Edulus is one of the easiest fungi in the forest to distinguish, as well as being one of the tastiest. Like all of the Boletus family, it has sponge-like tubes or pores instead of gills underneath the cap—something which immediately sets it apart from most mushrooms and toadstools in the forest. No fungi with this feature are really poisonous; a few can cause gastric upsets but these all have very distinct reddish or purplish tinged stems or cap undersides. So if we are careful about this one feature, we can do ourselves no harm, even if we do happen to confuse Boletus Edulus with another toadstool of the same family. But there's no real need for this either. The size of Boletus Edulus (it grows to eight or more inches in breadth) distinguishes it easily. It has a heavy, thick, velvet-brown cap, whiteish to olive-yellow pores, and a swollen-looking, pale brown stem covered with a network of white veins. You'll find it most commonly in beech woods, thrusting upwards from among the dead leaves, startingly large yet perfectly proportioned—almost too beautiful to eat. Grubs do not think so, however, so watch for their burrowings as you slice through the cap, particularly in older specimens.

BEET AND BOLETUS SOUP

½ cup finely chopped Boletus mushroom
1 small onion, finely chopped
Good pinch of dried thyme
2 cups water or potato-peeling stock
Juice of half a lemon or 2 Tbs. wine vinegar
4-5 small beets, whole and with about 1″ of their stem still on—this way they will retain colour when boiling.
1 Tbs. brown sugar
Salt, freshly ground black pepper
Little butter for sautéing

Heat the butter and sauté onions and mushrooms with a little salt and pepper, and the thyme. When soft, add the water or stock, cover and simmer gently for about twenty to twenty-five minutes. Take the whole, washed beets and cook until tender in salted boiling water. When done, take them out and slip off their skins. Slice into sticks and put them into the mushroom broth, together with lemon or vinegar and the sugar. Season with salt and pepper and simmer gently for a few minutes to blend the flavours. Serve with Potato Dumplings (p. 203) and a dollop of yoghurt or sour cream.

CABBAGE SOUP

1 onion, chopped
2 cups shredded cabbage
1 small potato, grated with peel
2 Tbs. butter
3 cups water
1 tsp. caraway seeds
1 tsp. salt
Dash of wine vinegar

Melt butter in large saucepan and add onion, potato and cabbage. Cover and cook for about ten to fifteen minutes; gradually add the water whilst stirring, and all the seasonings. Cook for about thirty minutes. Serve with sour cream or yoghurt.

CHESTNUT AND POTATO SOUP

1 large potato, grated with peel (or about 3 cups potato stock)
1 lb. fresh chestnuts
2 Tbs. butter
1 Tbs. flour
¼ cup red wine
Salt, pepper
Some grated nutmeg

Cook the potato in salted water. Meanwhile bake the chestnuts by placing them in a moderately hot oven (350° F) for about fifteen minutes, or until they can be pierced easily. Peel the chestnuts and chop or put through a grinder. Add them to the soup stock (should be about three cups) and simmer slowly for thirty minutes.

Melt the butter in another saucepan; blend in the flour and slowly add the soup, whisking all the while. When it is well blended, add the wine and the seasonings. Simmer for another five minutes or so and serve with a crispy Herbed Bread (p. 204).

CREAM OF CELERY SOUP

4-6 stalks of celery, with tops
1 small onion, chopped fine
3 cups milk
1 tsp. salt
3 Tbs. butter
2 Tbs. flour
1 cup cream
2 Tbs. soya sauce

Chop the celery up fine and cook, with the chopped onion, in the milk in a double boiler for fifteen minutes. Remove onion and celery. Melt butter in a saucepan, blend in flour and then slowly add the celery broth, whisking all the while. Add the celery, spices, onion and cream, and cook over a very low heat until smooth and slightly thickened. Add the soya sauce, blend, and serve.

CREAM OF MUSHROOM SOUP

½ lb. mushrooms, Boletus if possible
2 Tbs. flour
1 cup cream

2 pts. chicken broth
4 Tbs. butter
Salt, pepper
Grated nutmeg

Melt half the butter in heavy saucepan, add the very finely chopped mushrooms, cover and let simmer for about ten to fifteen minutes. Add to the soup stock, and cook for a further fifteen minutes. Melt remaining butter in saucepan; blend in flour, then slowly add the soup stock, whisking constantly. Add cream and seasonings and heat, but do not let it boil. Serve with a little chopped parsley in each bowl.

CREAM OF POTATO SOUP

3 potatoes, grated
1 onion, grated
3 Tbs. butter
2 Tbs. flour
1 Tbs. salt
1 bay leaf
½ teaspoon ground cummin
Salt, pepper
1½ pts. milk, scalded
Chopped parsley to garnish

Cook the potatoes and onion in just enough water to cover; the potatoes should be a thick mash. (Two cups of mashed potatoes can be substituted.) Add the scalded milk, to which the cummin and bay leaf has been added. Set aside while you melt butter in heavy saucepan; blend in flour, then slowly add the milk mixture, whisking constantly. Add salt and pepper and cook a further five minutes. Remove bay leaf, add chopped parsley and serve hot.

GREEN CREAM SOUP

Around this time of year we suddenly find we still have lettuces which have stood a bit too long so we don't want to use them for salad. This is an excellent way of using them up.

1 large head Cos lettuce (or 2 smaller heads of lettuce or 1 lb. any greens)
1 pt. chicken broth or vegetable stock
2 cups white sauce

Finely chop and cook your greens or, if using the

lettuce, simply cut fine or shred. Add to the stock and boil five minutes; add two cups white sauce and season to taste. Some paprika and a dash of cayenne pepper are good.

THICK PEPPER SOUP

- 2 green or red peppers, finely chopped
- 4-6 ripe tomatoes, skinned and chopped
- 1 onion, chopped
- 2 cups water
- 3 Tbs. butter
- 3 Tbs. flour
- 1 cup cooked groats
- Salt, black pepper
- 2 tsp. chopped lemon balm
- Sour cream or yoghurt for garnish

If you have a blender, put the pepper, tomatoes and onion through it and then add to the water. If not, chop the vegetables and cook until tender in the water. They can now be Moulied if you wish, or passed through a sieve (although personally, I like a few lumps and bumps of vegetables in my soups so never bother).

Melt the butter in a saucepan and blend in the flour; add the vegetable broth to this, slowly, whisking all the while. Season with the salt and pepper and cook until thickened. Now add the groats and cook a few minutes more to heat through. Add the lemon balm and serve with a dollop of yoghurt or sour cream in each bowl.

VEGETABLE SOUP

- 2 onions, diced
- 3 Tbs. butter
- 3-4 cups water or broth
- 2-3 cups mixed vegetables (peas, broad beans, runner beans, cabbage, turnip)
- 2 carrots, grated
- 2 tsp. salt
- Some ground black pepper
- 3 potatoes, diced
- 2 tomatoes, skinned and chopped
- Handful of fresh dill, chopped, or 2 Tbs. dried
- 1 cup milk

Sauté onions in butter and add the carrots and mixed vegetables, water, salt and pepper. Cover and cook over a low heat for about ten minutes. Add the potatoes, tomatoes, and the dill and cook a further twenty to twenty-five minutes. Stir in the milk and simmer a moment to heat through.

ITALIAN VEGETABLE SOUP

3 cups of diced or chopped vegetables which could include: celery, courgette, tomatoes, potatoes, peas, beans and onion
3 Tbs. olive oil
A good pinch each of basil, oregano, sage
2 cloves garlic, crushed
Handful of broken spaghetti
Salt, black pepper
Grated cheese

Heat oil in heavy skillet and add onion, and herbs. When onion is soft, add the rest of the vegetables and the garlic, salt and pepper. Toss to coat, then add about two to three cups of water. Simmer gently for twenty minutes or until all is done. (If you are using potatoes, add these first and cook for about ten minutes, then add the rest of the vegetables.) Add the broken spaghetti and cook for another ten minutes or a little longer if you like your spaghetti softer. Serve hot with a sprinkling of grated cheese in each bowl.

ORIENTAL STYLE VEGETABLE SOUP

½ cup each of the following: sliced mushrooms, bean sprouts, sliced celery, diced carrots, peas
2 rashers bacon, chopped or 1 Tbs. oil
1 tsp. grated ginger root
1 tbs. dry sherry
1 tsp. salt
6 cups water or broth
2 eggs, beaten

Combine bacon (or oil), ginger, sherry and sliced mushrooms and cook, stirring well, for about five to ten minutes. Add peas and carrots, some of the water, and simmer for another ten minutes. Add celery and sprouts, the rest of the water and the salt and cook a further five to ten minutes. Mix in the beaten eggs, stirring constantly, and heat until the egg is set in shreds. Serve with soya sauce and some chopped watercress.

MAIN COURSES

Aubergines

BAKED AUBERGINE

3 medium aubergines
1 green pepper, diced
2 onions, chopped
3 tomatoes, skinned and diced
¼ cup olive oil
1 clove garlic, minced
Salt, pepper
1 tsp. chopped basil
2 Tbs. chopped parsley

Cut aubergines lengthwise in half and scoop out the flesh, leaving about a quarter-inch in so that the aubergines don't collapse. Dice up the aubergine flesh and sauté in half of the heated olive oil with the pepper. Toss to coat the vegetables and season with salt and pepper and the minced garlic. Cook for about five minutes or until mixture is soft; divide among the six aubergine shells, gently pressing it down. Mix the onion, parsley, basil and the tomatoes; sauté in the remaining oil, mixing well, for about three to four minutes. Now spread this mixture on top of the aubergines, pressing down so that the shells are full but none of the mixture is spilling out. Arrange in a greased baking dish, topping with

some chopped hazel nuts
a little melted butter
some grated cheese

mixed into a paste. (A little milk may have to be added if it threatens to be too sticky.) Spread this on top of the aubergines. Bake in a moderate oven (350°F) for about forty minutes or so. Delicious served with a thyme-seasoned wheat or groat dish.

CURRIED AUBERGINE

1 large or 2 small aubergines
2-3 potatoes
1 onion, sliced
3 Tbs. butter
1 cup shelled broad beans
1 cup (or more) water
½ cup yoghurt
2 tsp. curry powder or
½ tsp. cummin seeds
½ tsp. coriander seeds
½ tsp. mustard seeds
1 tsp. tumeric
Pinch of cayenne pepper

Cut aubergine in very thin slices; sprinkle with salt, pile slices on a plate and cover with a weight to draw out the juice. Let stand for about an hour. This is necessary so that the aubergine will not take up too much of the fat in frying and become soggy.

Heat the butter in a skillet; add your curry powder or your curry spices with a good pinch of salt and stir, blending. Add onion and potato (which has been cubed), toss them to cover. Add a little of the water and cover to cook for about fifteen to twenty minutes.

Meanwhile, take the aubergine and dredge the slices in a little flour; add to the onion and potatoes, along with the broad beans and more water. Stirring often, cook for another fifteen minutes; add yoghurt and continue stirring for a further five to ten minutes. Delicious served with a salad and *Pidé* (pp. 211-12).

GREEK AUBERGINE, 'MOUSAKÁ'

Prepare batter for this dish as follows: Combine two beaten egg yolks with half a pint of milk and some salt and pepper. Cook gently, stirring constantly, and when it begins to thicken fold in the two egg whites which have been beaten stiff. Cook further until thickened to custard consistency. Let cool while you prepare the following:

1 lb. minced beef and/or mutton, seasoned with salt, black pepper
4 aubergines, cut and drained (as above) and dredged with flour
2-3 sliced onions
Olive oil—about ¼ cup
1 cup Tomato Sauce (p. 201)

Firstly, brown the meat in some of the oil. Set aside. Now, in a little more of the oil, fry the aubergines to get them a little crisp. Lastly, take the remainder of the oil and soften the onions in it.

Grease a deep-sided cake tin and cover the bottom with aubergines, the aubergines with some of the meat, the meat with some of the onions, and so on, ending with meat. Pour over one cup of tomato sauce and then make a lid of the batter. Bake in a moderate oven for about one hour. Serve with a side dish of yoghurt.

STUFFED AUBERGINES, TURKISH STYLE

3 medium aubergines
½ cup cooked wheat
½ cup minced cooked mutton
1 tomato, skinned and chopped
2 onions, chopped
¼ cup chopped hazel or walnuts
1 tsp. dried mint
½ tsp. marjoram
Salt, black pepper
Juice of 1 lemon
2-3 Tbs. olive oil

Cut the tops off the aubergines and scoop out the flesh, leaving about a quarter-inch so that the sides don't collapse. Dice the flesh, and mix with meat, wheat, tomato, the onion which has been sautéd in some oil, the nuts and seasonings.

Stuff the aubergines and replace their lids—with the stem-side down. Place in a pan with some olive oil, pour over about one cup of hot water and simmer gently for thirty minutes. Squeeze over the juice of a lemon, add more hot water to just cover, and simmer for a further thirty minutes. Serve with seasoned wheat and a side dish of yoghurt.

Cabbage

Cabbage is one of the most versatile of all the vegetables and deserves to fare much better in British cuisine. It can be simple or elaborate—we save the stuffed cabbage for special occasions.

GREEN CABBAGE WITH CARAWAY AND SOYA SAUCE

Heat some oil in a heavy pot and add a sliced onion; brown lightly and add caraway seed, and a good quantity of shredded cabbage. Toss to coat; sprinkle with freshly grated black pepper and a good tablespoon or so of soya sauce. Cover pot tightly and let it simmer for about ten minutes when the cabbage should be done, but still crunchy. This is delicious served with a savoury wheat or groats dish, accompanied with sour cream or yoghurt.

RED CABBAGE WITH WINE AND APPLE

1 head cabbage, thickly shredded
1 large sour apple, chopped
1 large onion, sliced
½ cup red cooking wine
Salt, freshly ground pepper
Oil (or butter) for cooking
Bay leaf
3-4 cloves

Heat enough oil to coat bottom of pan (or about two tablespoons butter); sauté onion with bay leaf and cloves until onion is transparent. Add cabbage, salt, pepper and chopped apple; place cover on pot and cook until tender--about twenty minutes.

Before serving, pour over red wine and place on gentle heat for two to three minutes; serve immediately.

This is excellent served with whole chestnuts sautéd to a golden brown in butter with potatoes and parsley.

RED CABBAGE, SWEET AND SOUR

1 head cabbage, shredded
2 sour apples, chopped
1 tsp. grated ginger root
1 cup water
1 tsp. salt
2 tbs. butter
1 rounded Tbs. cornflour
¼ cup wine vinegar
2 Tbs. brown sugar
½ tsp. salt or soya sauce to taste

Cook the cabbage and apple in the cup of water with the salt and ginger for about fifteen minutes. Meanwhile, prepare the sauce by heating the butter in a large saucepan, blending in the flour, then the wine vinegar, sugar and salt or soya sauce. To this add the cooked cabbage, adding more water if the sauce is too thick.

Serve over groats with side dishes of Pickled Cherries and Spiced Gooseberries (pp. 108-10).

EAST EUROPEAN-STYLE CABBAGE

1 green cabbage, coarsely shredded
4 Tbs. butter
Salt to taste
1 Tbs. dill seed
Coarsely ground black pepper
1 egg
1 cup sour cream (or yoghurt)

Cook cabbage in the butter over gentle heat for about fifteen minutes, stirring frequently so it doesn't stick. Stir in salt, dill seeds and cook a further five minutes. Beat the egg and sour cream together and add to the cabbage, mixing steadily until it begins to thicken.

Serve with wheat or groats, or with baked potatoes and meat patties, or with Broad Egg Noodles (pp. 205-6).

CABBAGE AND NOODLES

1 medium cabbage, shredded
4 Tbs. butter
Salt and pepper to taste

1 onion, sliced
1 Tbs. poppy seeds
3-4 cups Noodles (pp. 205-6)

Melt the butter in heavy pot and sauté the onion and poppy seeds together; add the shredded cabbage, salt and pepper, and cook, stirring often, until cabbage is lightly browned. Add the cooked noodles and toss to cover all with the seeds and butter, and to blend the tastes.

STUFFED CABBAGE

1 head cabbage
2 eggs
1 onion, grated
2 cups cooked wheat
2 tsp. salt
1 cup currants
4 Tbs. butter
1 onion, sliced
2 cups boiling water
2-3 tomatoes, skinned and chopped
2 Tbs. Dry Sherry (pp. 223-4)
1 Tbs. honey
Small piece of cinnamon bark

Pour a little boiling water over the cabbage and let it stand for about ten minutes. This should loosen the leaves enough so that they can be gently removed and are pliable. Remove the top eighteen leaves (or more, if the cabbage is a small one).

To the cooked wheat, add the beaten eggs, the grated onion, one teaspoon of the salt and half of the currants. Place a heaped tablespoon or so on each leaf and carefully roll up. If the ribs of the cabbage are thick and unwieldy, carefully cut them out before stuffing the leaf.

Melt butter in heavy, deep saucepan and lightly brown the onions. Add the rolled cabbage leaves, arranging them carefully, and the chopped tomatoes. Mix the honey, sherry and water together and pour this into the pot, adding the cinnamon. Cover tightly and gently simmer for about forty-five minutes.

If you have some stuffing left over, stuff green peppers with it, or some tomatoes. Serve with a little seasoned wheat (the stuffing is quite substantial) and yoghurt or sour cream on the side.

CABBAGE, MACROBIOTIC STYLE

1 medium cabbage, shredded
1 onion, sliced
1 Tbs. oil
¼ cup sesame, pumpkin or sunflower seeds
Good pinch of salt
2 Tbs. miso

Heat large skillet and add the seeds to roast. When they begin to pop, add the oil and onion, cooking for a few minutes. Add the cabbage and cook a further five minutes. Finally add the miso softened with a little water, the salt, and cook, tossing to coat the cabbage and blend the flavours, five minutes more. The resulting cabbage is very crunchy with a good bodied flavour, making a very delicious and nutritious meal if served over seasoned wheat.

CABBAGE WITH CHESTNUTS

1 medium cabbage, coarsely shredded
½ lb. chestnuts
½ cup butter
1 Tbs. flour
Salt to taste
Grated nutmeg

Pierce chestnuts and place in saucepan; cover with boiling water and simmer until outer and inner skins can be removed—about five minutes. Chop chestnuts and brown them in two tablespoons of the butter.

Heat the rest of the butter, add one tablespoon of the flour and let brown slightly. Add one cup of liquid from the cabbage and let cook until smooth. Add the chestnuts and the cabbage. Heat through, grate some nutmeg on top, season, and serve with a wheat or groats dish.

CARROTS AND BURDOCK, WITH BOLETUS

Burdock is one of our favourite wild foods and it is certainly plentiful—no matter where you live I think you can't be too far from it. Although some recommend eating the greens, we find them bitter. But the roots are exquisite and add a kind of energizing zest to a dish.

1 onion, sliced
1 medium-sized burdock root, well scrubbed
½ cup Boletus Mushrooms (see p. 113) finely cut
4-5 carrots, scraped and cut into sticks
Butter for frying
Salt and pepper to taste

In a heavy skillet melt some butter and sauté the onion and mushrooms together for about five minutes. Add the burdock root (sliced into rounds), more butter and a drop of water if necessary, and cook for about fifteen minutes. Add carrots, salt and pepper, and more water. Cook a further fifteen minutes, stirring often. The mushrooms should have formed a nice thick sauce for the burdock, onion and carrot.

This is superb served with seasoned wheat and a side dish of watercress salad.

CARROT AND POTATO CHARLOTTE

1 cup grated carrots
¾ cup water
3 cups grated, drained potatoes
3 eggs, separated, the yolks beaten and the whites stiffly beaten
4 Tbs. water biscuits, crumbled
2 tsp. salt
1 tsp. grated ginger root root
4 Tbs. melted butter

Cook carrots in the water for fifteen minutes and let cool. Mix potatoes, egg yolks, biscuit crumbs, salt, ginger and the butter into the carrots (which have not been drained). Fold in the beaten egg whites and turn into large greased baking dish. Bake in a moderate oven (350° F) for about an hour and serve hot.

CAULIFLOWER WITH BOLETUS MUSHROOM

1 medium-sized cauliflower
½ cup thinly sliced Boletus Edulus Mushrooms (see p. 113)
2 cloves garlic, minced
Salt and/or soya sauce to taste
2 Tbs. butter

Heat butter in a heavy skillet. Add garlic and thinly sliced mushrooms, sprinkling with salt and/or soya sauce. Cover and cook for about thirty minutes, checking every so often to make sure the mushrooms are not sticking--you may have to add a little water. Add cauliflower which has been cut up, including the stems. (Or, if you prefer, use a large cauliflower, cutting off the stems and saving for soup, using only the flowerettes for this recipe.) Sprinkle with salt and toss so all is blended. Cook for a further fifteen minutes, adding water if necessary. Absolutely marvellous served with mashed potatoes over which some cheese has been grated.

CAULIFLOWER, MACROBIOTIC-STYLE

1 medium-sized cauliflower
1 clove garlic, chopped
¼ cup sesame seeds
1 Tbs. oil

Cook cauliflower in salted boiling water for about eight minutes; it should only be partially cooked. Separate flowerettes and stalks. In a heavy skillet, heat the sesame seeds until they begin to pop. Now add the oil and garlic, heat, and finally the cauliflowerettes (the stalks and any leaves to be used for soup), mashing them with a fork, and turning constantly, until everything is well browned. Delicious served with noodles and a salad.

CAULIFLOWER CURRY

This makes a large quantity but it keeps well and, like many highly seasoned dishes, is better for the keeping.

2 medium cauliflowers
4 Tbs. butter
2 heaped tsp. curry powder or, preferably, make your own with the following ingredients in equal amounts:
cummin seeds
mustard seeds
coriander seeds
cardamon seeds
cayenne pepper
grated ginger root
turmeric
salt
cinnamon
1 clove garlic, crushed
½ cup water
2 cups broad beans, shelled
3 tomatoes, skinned and diced

Break up the cauliflowers into bite-sized pieces. Heat the butter and add all the spices or the curry powder. Stir until mixture is thoroughly heated; add the cauliflower and the broad beans, stir to coat the vegetables, and add the water. Cover and cook for about fifteen minutes or until the cauliflower and beans are tender. Add the tomatoes, stir well and serve as soon as the tomatoes have heated through. Serve with baked Tic Beans (p. 160) and *Pidé* (pp. 211-2).

BRAISED CELERY OVER MASHED POTATOES

We find that celery, once it has been standing in the garden for a while, will have rather tough outer stalks. This can be true of celery from the greengrocers' also. We don't particularly like it that way raw, so this is a good way of using up those tough stalks.

Cut up the tough stalks into one-inch pieces and sauté in some butter until browned. Soften some miso with water and add to the celery, stirring well.

Grease a casserole and line with left-over, softened, mashed potatoes; top with the celery mixture and bake for about twenty minutes to heat the potato; grate some cheese on top and return to the oven for a few minutes to melt the cheese.

CHESTNUTS AND PRUNES

½ lb. chestnuts
½ lb. prunes
½ tsp. cinnamon
Salt and pepper to taste

Pierce chestnuts and place in saucepan; cover with boiling water and simmer until outer and inner skins can be easily removed—about five minutes.

Meanwhile, have prunes soaking (at least an hour) and then cook until tender with a little lemon juice.

Combine the prunes and chestnuts, add salt, pepper and cinnamon and cook a few minutes to blend flavour.

Delicious served with a crunchy cabbage and wheat spiced with a dash of ginger.

Kebabs

Kebabs can be skewered chunks of meat, interspersed with onion, tomato, pepper and potato and cooked in open fires. They can be spiced minced meat, rolled in spiced flour, and fried until crisp. Finally, kebabs can be those very elaborate rolls of meat roasted upright and sliced cross-wise, served over flat bread with spicy yoghurt. But for the purposes of this book I'll just give some recipes for the minced meat kebabs.

INDIAN-STYLE KEBABS

1 lb. minced beef
1 or 2 onions, grated
1 tsp. salt
½ teaspoon grated ginger root
1 tsp. turmeric
1 tsp. ground coriander seed
½ tsp. coarsely ground black pepper
1 cup yoghurt
Flour for drenching
3 Tbs. butter (approx.) for frying

Mix together the meat, onion and spices and form into long sausage shapes. Dip into the yoghurt, then the flour, and fry in hot butter. Serve with seasoned groats, or baked tic beans and *Pidé* (pp. 211-12).

TURKISH-STYLE KEBABS

1 lb. minced mutton
1 or 2 onions, grated
2 tbs. chopped parsley
1 tsp. ground cummin
½ tsp. cayenne pepper
Salt to taste
1 cup yoghurt
Flour for drenching
Butter for frying

Mix together and prepare as Indian style kebabs. Serve on *Pidé* (pp. 211-12) over which is poured some melted butter and lastly a little yoghurt, in which freshly ground pepper is mixed.

AMERICAN-STYLE HAMBURGER

1 lb. ground beef
1 grated onion
Some stale bread, softened with milk
1 Tbs. dillweed
1 clove garlic, crushed
Salt, pepper
Flour for drenching
Oil for frying

Mix all the ingredients (except flour and oil) and form into patties. Drench with the flour and fry in hot oil until brown on both sides. Serve with, of course, chips and a variety of pickles and relishes for a real down-home feast.

JAPANESE-STYLE KEBABS

Or so a friend of ours says. I have my doubts as to its origins, but the taste is delicious.

1 lb. ground beef
1 grated onion
4 stalks of celery, finely chopped
¼ cup cooked mushrooms
¼ cup beer
3 Tbs. soya sauce
1 tsp. grated ginger root
Pepper
Flour for drenching
Oil for frying

Mix all the ingredients except the flour and oil. If it

seems a little sticky and threatens not to roll into balls, add some flour. Now roll into balls, roll in some flour to coat, and fry until nice and crisp in hot oil. They're delicious with a seasoned groat and wheat dish and a salad.

KOHL RABI AND POTATO

In a heavy skillet, dry-roast some sesame seeds until they begin to pop; now add some butter and your kohl rabi which has been cubed small. Toss well to coat and cook, adding a little water if necessary.

In a buttered casserole arrange a ring of mashed potatoes which have been cooked with a bay leaf; in centre place the kohl rabi and sesame seed mixture. Grate some cheese over the potato, pop under grill to melt, and serve garnished with watercress and with a watercress and carrot salad.

ONIONS, HERÁULT STYLE

When living in southern France we once had onions in a farmhouse cooked very simply, but deliciously.

In front of an open fire (can be coal) place unpeeled onions—they should be just near enough to get hot, without burning completely. During the evening, as you sit by your fire, just every now and then turn the onions so that they get done evenly. When they are hot, and feel soft, serve them with grilled cheese sandwiches and a salad for a late supper. Pass around plenty of butter, salt and a pepper mill for the onions.

RAGOÛT OF VEGETABLES

1 onion, chopped
1 aubergine, chopped (not sliced)
2 courgettes or 1 marrow, sliced
1 cucumber, diced
1 green pepper, sliced
4 Tbs. olive oil
2 cloves garlic
1 bay leaf
1 cup vegetable broth or water
2 tomatoes, skinned and diced

In a heavy skillet warm the oil (it should not be too hot for the vegetables should remain soft), and toss in the onions, garlic, bay leaf and the green pepper. Cook until pepper turns bright green, then add the courgettes or marrow, and the aubergine, and cook a further ten to fifteen minutes with the lid on. Now add the salt, pepper and the cucumbers; top with the vegetable broth and stir. The broth should almost evaporate by the time the vegetables are soft, but not falling apart—in about forty-five minutes. Serve hot with crusty bread.

SALSIFY WITH WHEAT

Salsify has a lovely delicate flavour but is, unfortunately, difficult to come by in the shops. However, it is easily grown and stands well throughout the winter in your garden.

For every four roots, use one onion and one carrot. Peel your onion and scrub the roots well. Cut salsify into two-inch lengths and drop into boiling water to cook until just tender.

Meanwhile, melt some butter in a skillet and sauté the onion and the carrot. Add the salsify which has been drained, and cook until nicely browned. Serve with wheat in which a good quantity of American cress or watercress has been chopped. Scorzonera can be cooked the same way.

SALADS

This is the season I start grating, chopping or shredding vegetables for salads. It's a good idea to add any leafy vegetable, however, when these are available.

APPLE, CELERY AND NUT SALAD

Combine equal amounts of diced apple and chopped celery with half the amount of crumbled walnuts or hazelnuts. Pour over a Mayonnaise Dressing (pp. 198-9). Delicious served as a salad or as a topping for open toasted sandwiches.

BEET SALAD

2 cups grated cooked beetroots
4 Tbs. grated horseradish
1 tsp. salt
1 tsp. caraway seeds, pounded slightly
2 tsp. vinegar
2 Tbs. vegetable oil

Combine all the ingredients together and chill for at least two hours.

BEETROOT AND CAULIFLOWER SALAD

1 cauliflower
1 large, or 2 small, cooked beetroots
French Dressing (p. 197)
Mayonnaise (pp. 198-9)
Watercress (or American cress)

The cauliflower can be partially cooked or raw; our family prefers it raw and crunchy. Separate the flowerettes from the stalks; the stalks can be shredded for this salad or reserved for soups. Pour French dressing over the cauliflower and chill.

Dice beets and in separate bowl pour French dressing over them and also chill.

When ready to serve, prettily arrange the cauliflower and beets in a bowl. Pour over mayonnaise dressing, garnish with plenty of cress.

BORAGE, COMFREY AND CABBAGE

1 small head cabbage, thinly shredded
1 cup each, finely chopped, borage comfrey
1 small onion, thinly sliced
Toasted Seed Dressing (p. 198)

Combine all the vegetables in a bowl and mix well. Pour over a toasted seed dressing and let stand for about an hour before serving. Toss again immediately before serving.

COLESLAW

4 cups shredded cabbage (about 1 medium cabbage)
½ cup grated carrot (about 2 medium carrots)
1 green pepper, thinly sliced
¼ cup water
¾ cup Cider Vinegar (p. 196)
½ cup Mayonnaise (pp. 198-9)
Pinch sugar
2 tsp. salt
Ground black pepper
½ tsp. celery seed
Pinch of mustard powder

Toss together the cabbage, carrots, green pepper. Gradually stir the water and vinegar into the mayonnaise. Add the seasonings and pour the dressing over the vegetables and toss until well mixed. Chill for about an hour before serving. This salad keeps very well.

RED CABBAGE SLAW

1 red cabbage, shredded
3 cups boiling water
1 Tbs. salt
⅓ cup vegetable oil
¼ cup Wine Vinegar (p. 196)
Pinch sugar, ground black pepper
1 medium onion, sliced
1 medium cooking apple, grated

Pour boiling water and salt over the shredded cabbage; let stand for ten minutes then drain.

Mix together the oil, vinegar, sugar and black pepper. Add onions and apple to the cabbage, then pour over the dressing and toss it well. Chill for about an hour before serving.

RED CABBAGE, CARROT AND WATERCRESS

Shred some cabbage and either treat as above, or leave raw. Grate an equal amount of carrot and add a good bunch of coarsely chopped watercress. Pour over a Stilton Cheese Dressing (p. 197) and toss well; chill for at least an hour and toss well again before serving.

CABBAGE ROSE SALAD

1 small solid white cabbage ('drumhead')
3-4 carrots, grated
3-4 stalks celery, chopped
2 boiled potatoes, diced
1 cup French Dressing (p. 197)
½ cup Mayonnaise (pp. 198-9)

Remove outer leaves of cabbage and cut stalk off close to the leaves; save stalk and outer leaves for soup or stock.

Cut out centre of cabbage with a sharp knife, making a large 'bowl' out of the cabbage. Place this 'bowl' in iced water while you prepare rest of salad.

Shred remaining cabbage and combine with the celery, carrots and potatoes. Toss well in the French dressing and let marinade for an hour or so. Now fill the 'bowl' with this mixture. (Be sure to drain the cabbage 'bowl' well.) Chill and, when ready to serve, pour over the mayonnaise. Garnish with parsley, cress or sliced green or red peppers.

PEPPER SALAD

8 green or red peppers
2 tsp. salt
½ tsp. grated black pepper
2 cloves garlic, chopped
1 bay leaf
1 cup Cider Vinegar (p. 196)
¼ cup water

Cut peppers in half; discard seeds and white fibres and slice evenly. Combine the rest of the ingredients in a saucepan and bring to the boil; pour over the sliced peppers; chill for a few hours; remove bay leaf and serve.

This salad will keep well for a few days.

KOHL RABI WITH NUTS

Grate a kohl rabi in a bowl; mix well with about half a a cup chopped walnuts or hazelnuts. Toss in a Yoghurt Dressing (p. 198) and chill before serving.

PICKLED VEGETABLE SALAD

2 finely diced green peppers
1 or 2 grated onions
3 cups coarsely grated beets
3 cups grated cabbage
1 Tbs. salt
2 cups Cider Vinegar (p. 196)
1 tsp. sugar
2 Tbs. mustard seed
1 Tbs. celery seed
Small sprig rosemary

Combine all the ingredients in a saucepan and bring to the boil; cook for ten minutes, mixing occasionally.

Pour into clean hot jars and seal. Cool, then chill for two days before serving. The salad will, of course, keep well for a few days in a cool place.

DESSERTS

AUTUMN PUDDING

1 large cooking apple
1 lb. fresh blackberries
½ cup water
¾ cup brown sugar
½ tsp. mixed spice
Enough stale, thinly sliced bread to completely line pudding basin

Core apple and slice thinly; put in a saucepan with water and berries and simmer until tender. Stir in sugar and spice and allow to cool.

Meanwhile, grease a pudding basin and line the bottom with the thinly sliced bread; trim it and make sure that all of the sides and bottom of the basin are covered. Place in a layer of fruit, then a layer of bread, pressing it down gently; then a layer of fruit and so on until all are used up, ending with some bread. Place a closely fitting plate on top and weigh it down. Store in a cool place for about twelve hours or so; turn out and serve with either fresh cream or Custard (pp. 62-3).

BAKLAVA

This is a traditional Middle Eastern dessert, very rich in nuts, generally almonds, and honey.

1 cup blanched almonds (or walnuts and hazelnuts can be substituted)
½ cup butter
3 Tbs. honey
1 tsp. cinnamon
Puff Pastry (pp. 207-8)
¼ cup sugar
½ cup water mixed with 3 Tbs. honey
1 Tbs. lemon juice, plus extra lemon wedges for serving

Chop the almonds. Cream the butter, honey and cinnamon and add to the nuts.

Roll out puff pastry very thinly and cut into the shape of the high sided baking tin which you will use. Line the tin with aluminium foil and place one of the cut out shapes in it; spread with more of the mixture, top with some pastry and so on until you've used up the ingredients, but ending with a shape of pastry on the top. Bake in a hot oven (400°F) for about fifteen to twenty minutes.

Take out of the oven and pour over it the following mixture: gently heat the water with the sugar and honey and lemon—let it come to the boiling point and simmer a few moments to bind the flavours. Pour over the baked baklava and let it sit for about an hour, or until it is just cool. Eat with plenty of freshly squeezed lemon juice.

BEETROOT HELVA

4 medium beetroots
1 cup brown sugar, tightly packed
¼ cup butter
3 Tbs. ground walnuts
3 Tbs. chopped raisins or currants
1 tsp. cardamon powder (the crushed seeds from two pods)

Place beetroots in water and boil until tender; slip off the skins and mash until very smooth. Add sugar and cook over low heat, stirring constantly, until mixture thickens. Now gradually add the butter, stirring until all is dissolved and mixture is very thick. Take off the heat; add raisins or currants, nuts and cardamon, spread out on a plate and flatten. Cut into wedges when cool.

Blackberries

If you are collecting them from roadsides, be sure to wash them very, very well. They can then be used in any berry recipe—pies, tarts, etc. Below are some of our favourites.

BLACKBERRY PIE

4 cups blackberries
¾ cup brown sugar with
  1 Tsp. cinnamon
2 Tbs. flour
1 Tbs. chopped lemon
  balm
Grated nutmeg
Pie Crust Dough (p. 207)

Line a greased pie (flan) dish with half the dough; mix together the berries, sugar, flour, balm and nutmeg and fill the pie shell; roll out remaining dough and cover pie, sealing the edges well by fluting; slash the top, brush with milk and bake for forty-five minutes in a hot oven (400° F).

BLACKBERRY ROLL

Follow recipe for Gooseberry Roll (p. 104), substituting blackberries which have been sprinkled with cornflour, for the gooseberries.

BLACKBERRY AND APPLE CHARLOTTE

Line an ovenproof dish with two-thirds of Sweet Pastry (pp. 206-7), reserving the remainder of the pastry for the top of the Charlotte. The pastry must be patted firmly to line the bottom of your dish. Now fill with equal amounts of chopped apples and washed blackberries which have been tossed in flour.

Sprinkle the top with brown sugar; grate some nutmeg over the top and now pat the remaining dough into place—if it is too crumbly to pat into place, treat as a crumble topping. Bake in a moderate oven for about thirty minutes.

CARROT HELVA

2 lb. carrots, grated, cooked and drained
¼ cup water
1 cup brown sugar
¼ cup butter
2 cups ground walnuts hazelnuts, or almonds
½ tsp. nutmeg

Cook the sugar and water together until a thread is formed when a fork is lifted from the pan; stir in the cooked, drained carrots, stirring well, and cook until the syrup is absorbed—about ten minutes. Remove from heat and blend in the butter, nuts and nutmeg. Press into individual plates and serve hot or cold.

SWEET CARROTS FOR AFTERS

6 medium carrots
½ cup each
  stoned raisins
  dates
  roasted nuts
3 Tbs. honey
2 Tbs. butter

Gently melt butter in heavy saucepan; add sliced carrots (if carrots are cut into sticks it adds to the overall texture of the dish) and cook gently for a few minutes until the carrots begin to soften. Now add half a cup of water and cook until the carrots are soft; finally add the fruits, nuts and honey, cooking a further three minutes.

This dessert can be kept warm during the meal by placing in a greased ovenproof dish in a low oven. In our family, the children love it as it is, but the adults prefer a squeeze of lemon juice with it.

CARROT MINCE PIE

Here's another recipe for using carrots. It's a good tip to remember that you can substitute carrots for half the quantity of apples in many recipes—sometimes carrots can be substituted completely. It really depends on you and your family so it is best to experiment.

Line a flan tin with Sweet Pastry (pp. 206-7), pressing it down well. Then fill with the following mince:

1 cup grated carrots
1 cup stoned raisins
½ cup cooked wheat (or well chopped nuts)
½ cup brown sugar
1 tsp. cinnamon
½ tsp. grated nutmeg
½ tsp. grated ginger root
1 egg, beaten
4 Tbs. or so of butter

Melt the butter and cook the carrots until soft; add the raisins wheat, sugar and spices and mix thoroughly. Bind with the egg and put into the flan dish. Bake in a moderate oven (350°F) for thirty minutes. If the edges threaten to darken, cover with tin foil.

NUT PIE

This is a rather special pie which tastes delicious but needs to be made with care. For the pastry, you will need:

2 cups flour
1 egg
Pinch of salt
½ cup butter
½ cup sugar
2 Tbs. sherry

Sift together the flour, salt and sugar. Beat egg lightly. Blend ingredients, alternately, with butter in a deep bowl. Lastly, add the sherry, slowly, just enough to make a firm pastry. Roll out pastry into a circle and line a greased flan dish (nine- or ten-inch) with it. The remaining pastry should be rolled into strips for criss-crossing on the top.

Set aside and prepare the filling.

2 cups milk
2 eggs, beaten
½ cup chopped nuts (medium-fine if you're using a grinder)
3 Tbs. brown sugar
¾ cup wholewheat flour
½ tsp. grated nutmeg
Pinch of salt

Place flour in a deep saucepan and gradually blend in the milk until the mixture is very smooth. Add the sugar, eggs, salt and nutmeg and blend thoroughly. Cook gently over a medium heat, stirring constantly to prevent lumping and sticking. (It is best to use one of those flat, wooden implements with a hole through them—like flat spoons, hollow in the middle). Lower flame, still stirring, and cook for about ten minutes. Gradually add the nuts, still stirring until mixture is very smooth.

Remove from fire and cool. Pour filling into pastry shell; place strips criss-cross on top and bake in a moderately hot oven (375°F) for about forty-five minutes—or until filling is firm but not dry and pastry a lovely golden brown.

If you like, sprinkle with a little icing sugar just before serving.

NUT TARTS

Pastry (p. 206)
1 cup chopped nuts
1 cup chopped raisins
1 cup brown sugar
1 lemon—juice and rind
1 egg, beaten
1 Tbs. butter
1 Tbs. water

Line muffin tins with pastry, reserving a little to place criss-crosses on the top for decoration.

Mix together all the other ingredients, grating the lemon rind first, then squeezing in the juice. Fill the shells, decorate with criss-crisses on top, and bake in moderate oven (359°F) for about twenty-five minutes or until pastry is golden.

PRESERVING

Chutneys

APPLE CHUTNEY

5 lb. apples, cored and chopped
2 lb. onions, chopped
1 lb. raisins and dates, mixed and chopped
¾ lb. brown sugar
Bruised ginger root
Bay leaf
Salt
Cayenne pepper
3 cups (approx.) Spiced Vinegar (p. 196)

Combine the apples, onions, raisins, dates and sugar. Mix in salt (about one tablespoon or more), other spices to taste and cover with spiced vinegar. Simmer gently for about two hours, stirring frequently; put in clean jars and seal tightly. This is a good basic chutney, to which you can vary the ingredients according to taste.

MILD APPLE CHUTNEY

Reduce a number of apples to a pulp by baking slowly in an oven or coring and chopping, and simmering gently until soft. Add half as many cut up onions (or shallots) as apples. Spice with salt, turmeric, some mustard powder and about two tablespoons of brown sugar to every pint of apple and onion mixture. Simmer together in Spiced Vinegar (p. 196) just long enough for it all to form into a pulp and bottle when cold.

APPLE AND BEET CHUTNEY

- 8 large cooking apples, cored and chopped
- 2-3 beetroots, with their tops if possible
- 2 onions, chopped
- 1 teaspoon caraway seeds
- 1 teaspoon cayenne pepper
- 1 teaspoon, rounded, salt
- Spiced Vinegar (p. 196)

Cook beets with their tops in a small amount of salted water; slip off skins of beets and chop them, with their tops. Combine beets, tops, and left-over cooking water with chopped apples, onions and the spices. Cover with spiced vinegar and simmer gently for about one hour or so; bottle when cold. This is a lovely-looking chutney.

APPLE AND GREEN TOMATO CHUTNEY

- 2 lb. cooking apples, cored and chopped
- 2 lb. green tomatoes, chopped
- 1 cucumber, chopped
- 4 onions, sliced
- ½ lb. currants
- 1 lb. brown sugar
- 2 Tbs. mustard
- 2 tsp. grated ginger root
- 1 tsp. cayenne pepper
- 2 Tbs. salt
- Malt or homemade Fruit Vinegar (p. 196)

Place all the ingredients in a heavy saucepan and cover with the vinegar; simmer gently for two to three hours, stirring frequently; bottle when cool. We like this chutney crunchy, so cook it only for one-and-a-half or two hours; but most people tend to like their chutneys softer.

APPLE AND TURNIP CHUTNEY

2 lb. cooking apples, cored and chopped
2 lb. turnips, chopped
1 lb. onions, sliced
½ lb. currants
½ lb. brown sugar
1 Tbs. mustard
3 cloves garlic, chopped or crushed
1 tsp. cayenne pepper
1 rounded Tbs. salt
Malt vinegar or homemade Fruit Vinegar (p. 196)

Cook apples and turnips together until soft enough to mash; reserve cooking water for soup or sauces.

Put all the ingredients in a heavy saucepan, covering with vinegar, and simmer gently for at least an hour, stirring frequently. Bottle and cover when cool.

AUTUMN CHUTNEY

This is our favourite chutney because the whole family can help in collecting the blackberries and hazelnuts. However, if these are not available in your area, substitute raisins or currants for the berries and peanuts for the hazelnuts.

1 lb. brown sugar
1 Tbs. salt
¼ cup mustard seed
¼ cup coriander seed
¼ cup ginger root, grated coarsely
1 Tbs. red (chili) peppers
1 lb. blackberries
½ lb. shelled hazelnuts
¼ lb. garlic cloves
¼ lb. onions or shallots
2 pt. Malt vinegar or homemade Fruit Vinegar (p. 196)
20 large, sour, cooking apples

Place the berries and cored, quartered cooking apples in a large heavy pot or preserving pan and slowly bring apples to a pulp. Add chopped nuts, the sugar, vinegar, garlic, onions or shallots and spices. Boil together for about twenty minutes; put into clean hot jars and seal when cool.

This is an extremely hot, tasty chutney which will keep for about two years.

MIXED FRUIT CHUTNEY

This is another spicy, tangy, chutney using lots of dried fruit, and not so much sugar.

1 lb. cooking apples, cored and chopped
½ lb. blackberries
½ lb. gooseberries
¾ lb. currants
½ lb. chopped prunes
½ lb. dates, chopped
1 cup brown sugar
1 cup chopped mint leaves
1 rounded Tbs. salt
2 cloves garlic, minced
1 stick cinnamon
2 cups Spiced Vinegar (p. 196) or 2 cups Cider Vinegar and the following spices: 1 tsp. each
ground coriander
grated ginger root
black pepper
mustard powder

Combine all the ingredients in a large saucepan; bring to boil, and simmer gently, stirring frequently, for an hour. Bottle and cover when cool.

Pickles

PICKLED BEETS WITH CARAWAY

4 cups cooked beets, cold and sliced
2 tsp. salt
2 tsp. brown sugar
3 tsp. caraway seeds
2 cups Cider Vinegar (p. 196)

Bring to the boil the vinegar and spices; simmer gently for about ten minutes and cool.

Place beets in a crock or large glass jar; cover with the spiced vinegar; cover and store in a cool place.

PICKLED SPICED BEETROOT

Take beetroots and chop off the tops, leaving an inch or so of the green (this stops them from 'bleeding' so much). Reserve the tops for Relish (pp. 149-50). Cook beetroot until tender and skin them. If they are large, chop them into quarters, otherwise leave them whole.

To every three cups of beetroot water add one cup of brown sugar, two cups of cider vinegar, some cloves and a good pinch of mace. Let this come to the boil, then add beetroots. When they are thoroughly heated, put in jars and seal.

PICKLED CABBAGE

This is a cross between sauerkraut and pickled cabbage and, to our way of thinking, far superior to either. You can use any cabbage (even red is good) for this recipe, but the solid, white drumhead, normally used for sauerkraut, is best.

1 medium cabbage
1 cup, (approx.) salt
4-5 cloves garlic, chopped
2 cups chopped, fresh dill (stalks included) or
½ cup dill seeds
Cider Vinegar (p. 196)

Finely shred the cabbage; place in layers, salting well, in a crock or large glass sweet jar—or even an open bowl.

Press down after salting each layer, alternating with the dillweed or seeds. As you do this, the brine should begin to run if you are using the white drumhead cabbage. If not, you may have to pound to bring the brine to rise.

Leave for about three days while any scum may rise to the top, but do make sure that the brine covers the cabbage. When it has stopped working, place it in clean jars (don't drain it—just lift it out letting as much brine come with it as it wants) and cover with cider vinegar.

CRUNCHY PICKLED CARROTS

Arrange well-scrubbed carrots which have been cut lengthwise into quarters in clean warm jars; shove wedges of onion between, and stalks of dillweed. Pour over vinegar mixture to the following proportions:

1 cup salted water
3 Tbs. salt
2 cups Cider or Fruit Vinegar (p. 196) spiced with 1 tsp. black peppercorns
2 chili peppers

Keep at least one month in cool place before eating.

PICKLED SPICY CARROTS

2 lb. carrots
¼ cup mixed spices (cinnamon, mace, cloves)
2 cups vinegar
2 cups carrot water
4 cups brown sugar

Wash carrots; cut in half lengthwise, then chop into two-inch pieces; cook in salted water (one teaspoon salt per pint of water) until just tender. Drain.

Mix two cups of the cooking water from the carrots with the vinegar, spices and sugar; cook until boiled to a syrup. Add carrots and let simmer gently for about two hours; bottle while hot and seal.

PICKLED CAULIFLOWER WITH MUSHROOMS

In this pickle, the mushrooms are very soft, and the cauliflower very crunchy, so the whole has a nice interesting texture. We use Boletus Edulus (p. 113) mushrooms which impart their taste well. But, if using them, remember to chop them very fine.

Take equal amounts of mushrooms and chopped onions, combine with some salt and black pepper, and add just enough Cider or Fruit Vinegar (p. 196) to cover; let simmer gently for about an hour (or can be put into the lower rung of the oven while you're baking).

Separate the cauliflower into flowerettes, reserving the stalks for soup or relish; sprinkle liberally with salt and leave to stand overnight.

Rinse flowerettes in cold water and drain; place a layer in a crock or glass jar, cover with some of the mushrooms, then place a layer of cauliflower, then mushrooms, and so on, ending with cauliflower. Pour over the following vinegar mixture:

1 cup water, salted with 3 Tbs. salt
2 Tbs. dillseed
2 cups Cider or Fruit Vinegar (p. 196) spiced with 1 tsp. black peppercorns

Cover and keep about a month in a cool place before using.

DILL CUCUMBERS

Cucumbers
Chili peppers
Dillweed
Horseradish root
½ cup salt to 4 cups water

Scrub cucumbers and cut lengthwise into quarters. Arrange in clean jars, shoving small pieces of horseradish root between the cucumbers. Place lots of dillweed—stalks, flowers, everything—over each layer of cucumbers, adding a few pieces of chopped chili peppers. Now cover completely with the brine solution. Seal, but add more brine solution if the cucumbers rise. Watch also that the brine doesn't ooze out; if it does, cover with fresh brine and re-seal. Keep at least one month before using.

CUCUMBER MUSTARD PICKLES

If you can get hold of gherkin cucumbers for this recipe, do; we grow them in a cold frame up here so they should do well in the south. Ridge cucumbers can also be used, but in that case, slice or chop them.

Place your well scrubbed gherkins or chopped cucumbers in a crock or large glass jar. Cover with the following solution, weighing the cucumbers down with a plate.

2 cups Cider or Fruit Vinegar (p. 196)	¼ cup salt
1 cup water	¼ cup mustard powder
	½ cup brown sugar

Combine the dry ingredients; add vinegar gradually, stirring constantly to dissolve mustard. Add water and stir to mix thoroughly. Pour over the cucumbers.

This recipe has one great advantage if you are growing your own cucumbers—you can add to it. If you use a large crock, just fill it with as may cucumbers as you have and cover them with the mustard sauce, and weigh down; as you collect more cucumbers from your garden, add them, and cover with fresh sauce. Keep this pickle for several weeks before using it.

CUCUMBERS PICKLED WITH TARRAGON

This is another recipe for those growing their own herbs, for both the dill and the tarragon should be fresh.

12 cucumbers, cut in quarters lengthwise	Fresh dill—about 3-4 stalks
1 small horseradish root	½ cup salt
1 Tbs. white peppercorns	1 pt. water
6 bay leaves	2 pt. vinegar
Fresh tarragon—about one hefty stalk	½ cup mustard seed

Arrange the tarragon, dill, peppercorns, bay leaves and horseradish in clean jars as for preceding recipe. Place the mustard seeds in a muslin bag and put in with the cucumbers; make a brine of the salt, water and vinegar, beating it together and pour over the cucumbers to cover. Weigh down with a plate and keep in a cool place for about six weeks.

SALTED CUCUMBERS

This is a very simple way of keeping cucumbers which you can use in any oriental-style recipes.

Simply scrub well your cucumbers and pack them, whole, in jars. Cover with a brine (1 cup of salt to one pint of water) which has been boiled and skimmed to clear, and finally cooled.

CUCUMBER RELISH

- 2 firm cucumbers
- 2 cups finely-chopped celery
- 1 Tbs. salt
- ¼ cup sugar
- 2 Tbs. grated horseradish root
- 1 onion, well chopped
- 1 tsp. ground black pepper
- Vinegar to cover

Mix all the ingredients except the vinegar. Now add the vinegar and rapidly bring to the boil and simmer for about five minutes. Bottle while hot, adding vinegar as necessary to keep ingredients well covered. Seal.

This relish can be used immediately.

MIXED RELISH

This is an excellent recipe for using up turnip tops, beetroot tops, onion greens, tough celery stalks and those maddening last green tomatoes which always seem to appear after you've made your chutney or pickle.

4 cups cooked, minced beetroots, celery, green tomatoes, peppers, onion greens, etc.
½ cup grated horseradish root
2 tsp. salt
1 tsp. ground cummin or mustard powder
1 cup or more vinegar (with lemon juice added if you like)
2 Tbs. brown sugar

Combine the well-chopped vegetables with the horseradish; add the seasoning, sugar and all the vinegar the mixture will absorb. Bottle. This relish will keep extraordinarily well.

Incidentally, this relish can also be made with elderberries in place of half of the vegetables, which makes it a particularly tangy relish.

PICKLED NASTURTIUM SEEDS

Nasturtiums are not merely pretty faces. The leaves are excellent chopped in salads, as are the flowers. The flowers are less tangy than the leaves, but give a nice piquant flavour if added to sauces. The seeds, when ripe, are excellent pickled and used in place of capers. And, incidentally, the plant is loved by bees, but will deter other, unwanted, insects.

For pickling the seeds, simply pick nice firm green ones and place in a clean jar. Pour over Spiced Vinegar (p. 196); place some nasturtium leaves on top to hold down the seeds, making sure nothing is sticking out of the vinegar. Cover and leave for about six weeks.

PICKLED ONIONS

Pour boiling water over small white pickling onions to cover; let stand for two minutes, drain, cover with cold water and peel. Let stand in well-salted water overnight. Pour over cold water and drain while you prepare the following spiced vinegar. To every one pint of vinegar add:

¼ cup sugar
3 bay leaves
3 chili peppers
1 tsp. black peppercorns
2 cloves garlic, crushed
1 tsp. cummin seeds

Boil up the vinegar and spices and let simmer for a few minutes; add the onions and bring to the boil then pour at once into clean hot jars and seal.

PUMPKIN OR MARROW PICKLE

Pumpkins may not be at your local greengrocer's, but I notice that seeds are available from many seedsmen now. We can't grow them up here, but I'm including this recipe which I made in the States where pumpkins are plentiful. If you don't have pumpkins, try using marrow instead.

4 cups peeled, cubed pumpkin (or marrow)
¾ cup vinegar
¼ cup treacle
1 cup brown sugar
10 cloves
2 tsp. cinnamon
1 tsp. salt

Combine the pumpkin or marrow with the vinegar, treacle, and the seasonings in a saucepan. Bring to the boil and cook over low heat until pumpkin is translucent and easily pricked with a fork. Pack into sterile jars and seal. Keep in a cool place. This pickle only keeps for three to four months.

PICKLED GREEN TOMATOES

Firm, green tomatoes are delicious treated like cucumbers—follow recipe for either Dill Cucumbers or Cucumbers Pickled with Tarragon (pp. 147-8), substituting the green tomatoes for the cucumbers.

PICKLED WHITE TURNIPS

Last summer we grew far too many of the small white, purple-topped turnips and so I decided to try and pickle some. They were quite delicious, and kept well.

Simply scrub the turnips and slice thinly. Pack in clean jars, alternating layers with onions and dillweed. Pour over a vinegar and water combination as in the recipe for Crunchy Pickled Carrots (p. 146). Cover and keep at least one month before eating.

Relishes

BEETROOT AND HORSERADISH RELISH

- 3 cups cold, boiled beetroot, chopped well
- ½ cup horseradish root, grated
- ½ tsp. pepper
- 2 tsp. salt
- ¾ cup vinegar
- 1 Tbs. sugar (can be omitted, in which case add another teaspoon salt)

Combine all the ingredients except the vinegar and mix thoroughly. (Beetroot and horseradish can, of course, be put through a food blender for a smoother consistency.) Add enough vinegar to completely cover the mixture—the vinegar may settle so leave for a few hours, then add more. Be sure to add as much as the beetroot and horseradish will absorb. Cover and keep in cool place. This relish will keep for a long time and is excellent with cold meats.

TOMATO KETCHUP

This is a recipe that a friend of ours, living in a small mountain village in southern France, makes in a huge black pot over an open fire in one of those large, open-hearth fireplaces I always associate with Beatrix Potter illustrations. I've made the recipe on an ordinary stove with good results although I have to admit I enjoyed it more in southern France—something about the mingling of the smoking wood and cooking tomatoes and spices.

- 20 tomatoes (medium-sized)
- 1 cooking apple
- ½ cup brown sugar
- 1 scant tsp. cayenne pepper

3 onions	¼ cup mixed allspice and stick cinnamon
3 green peppers	1 pint Cider or Fruit Vinegar (p. 196)
2 cloves garlic	
2 bay leaves	
2 Tbs. salt	

Boil together the first seven ingredients until soft; strain through colander and then through a sieve (or pass the whole thing through your blender). Tie all the spices in bag; add sugar to strained vegetables, place bag in saucepan and boil the whole mixture rapidly, without scorching, for one-and-a-half hours, until thick, or reduced by about one half. Remove spice bag, add vinegar and boil for ten minutes longer, by which time the whole should be thick. If mixture will absorb more vinegar, add it, stirring and cooking, but making sure the mixture remains thick. Bottle while hot, and seal.

CARROT
PLONK

Chapter Five
Winter

SOUPS

During the winter months we have soup every day. Generally, it is made from the previous night's left-overs mixed with miso and garnished with fresh parsley or chives—both of which I have growing in our kitchen window. But at least once a week I start the soup fresh and the following are some hearty, warming soups for cold wintry days.

CREAM OF AMERICAN CRESS SOUP

'American' cress is sold by most seed merchants but not available at the greengrocer's to my knowledge. The greatest advantage it has over ordinary watercress is that it has a longer growing period. In fact, up here on Skye it grows all through the winter months, if somewhat slowly and unhappily at times.

2 onions, sliced thinly
1 cup American cress, chopped
1 Tbs. vegetable oil
$^1/_3$ cup oat flakes ('porridge oats')
1 tsp. salt
2 Tbs. soya sauce

Heat oil in heavy saucepan; add onions and cook until transparent; now add the oats, stirring well so that they become well coated; now slowly add water, stirring constantly, and bring to the boil. Add salt and let simmer about thirty minutes. Add cress and simmer a further five minutes; just before serving add the soya sauce, stirring well. to mix.

Celery can be substituted for the cress, in which case

double the amount, chop it fine, and add it after the onions. Cook until it changes colour, then add the oats and proceed as above.

CREAM OF ARTICHOKE SOUP

We grow a lot of Jerusalem artichokes—or, to be precise, some seasons back we planted some and now they keep coming up and up. People always seem to say something to the effect, 'Oh, Jerusalem artichokes are all right, but they're such a nuisance to peel. Why do you grow so many?'

Well, we grow them because we like them (and they tend to grow themselves, anyway), and, if you don't like peeling them, don't. I never have. Just scrub the roots well.

1 lb. Jerusalem artichokes
1 onion, sliced
1 Tbs. butter
1 cup water or stock
Salt, black pepper
Grated nutmeg
1 tsp. dried lemon balm
1 pt. milk

Melt butter in saucepan; add sliced onions and cook until they're transparent. Slice artichokes into the pot and stir well; add the water or stock and cook until the artichokes are soft. Mash them with a fork; add milk and seasonings and heat but do not boil.

BOSTON FISH CHOWDER

2 lb. white fish
4 potatoes, scrubbed and cubed (don't bother peeling unless you want to)
1 onion, sliced
3 rashers streaky bacon, chopped
2 Tbs. salt
1 tsp. ground black pepper
3 Tbs. butter
4 cups scalded milk

Cook fish in water until it is possible to skin and bone; discard bones, skin, head and tails if there are any. Cook bacon gently in heavy saucepan, rendering the fat; add onion and potatoes; cook with one cup of water for about seven minutes; add fish liquid, the fish, and let it all simmer for about ten minutes. Finally, add the scalded milk and stir in the butter.

Serve with water biscuits crumbled on top.

MUSSEL CHOWDER

Mussels are easily identified as clusters of metallic blue-grey bivalve molluscs clinging to rocks on the lower shore, particularly around river estuaries. They may also be found on the piles supporting jetties, etc. However, the *greatest* caution must be taken with mussels for of all shellfish they are the most likely to cause food poisoning. For this reason they should never be taken outside the autumn and winter months nor should they ever be taken near a sewage outlet or near any estuary that may be polluted.

Mussels should be treated by soaking in three changes of clean water—sea water is best—over three consecutive days. Immediately before cooking, any that are open or remain open when prised apart gently, should be discarded as dead. Once you're satisfied, scrub each one under the tap to remove tiny stones and bits of shell. Finally plunge the lot into salted boiling water and cook until the shells open and the flesh inside can be removed after cooling.

- 3 cups cleaned, cooked mussels
- 1 cup cooking water from mussels
- 4 cups diced potatoes
- 1 large onion, chopped
- 4 cups scalded milk
- 4 Tbs. butter
- 1 bay leaf
- 3 cloves garlic, crushed
- Salt, freshly ground black pepper

Melt butter in deep saucepan, sauté onion and garlic, salt, pepper and bay leaf, stirring constantly; add potatoes, mussel water and enough water to just cover the potatoes; cook until tender—about twenty minutes. Finally, add the milk and mussels, cooking gently just long enough to heat through.

Serve with a nice hot, crunchy bread or some freshly-baked scones.

HERRING SOUP, RUSSIAN STYLE

2 cups milk, scalded
2 herrings (previously soaked in cold water)
2 cups water
1 onion, chopped
1 teaspoon dill seed
Salt, black pepper to taste

Place water, onions, dill seed and salt and pepper in saucepan and boil for ten minutes; add herring which has been cut up into small pieces and cook until herring is tender. Add milk, heat through, and serve with dark bread.

This is obviously a soup for those who don't mind picking bones out from between their teeth! Our family is rather divided on the subject.

PARSNIP SOUP

3 good-sized parsnips
1 carrot
1 potato
1 onion, sliced
2 Tbs. butter
1 bay leaf
2 cups water (or stock)
2 cups milk
Salt, pepper
Good pinch of ground mace

Scrub the parsnips, carrots and potato and chop. (Don't peel them unless you really feel you must.) Sauté all the vegetables in the butter along with the bay leaf for about ten minutes, stirring frequently. Add the water and cook a further ten to fifteen minutes, adding the salt and pepper at this stage. Finally add the milk and the mace, cooking just long enough to heat through and blend the flavours. Serve garnished with some finely-chopped celery greens if available, or some of the parsnip greens.

POTATO SOUP

3 potatoes, scrubbed and diced
1 onion, chopped
1-2 stalks celery, chopped
1 Tbs. parsley, chopped
1 Tbs. caraway seed
2 Tbs. butter
Salt, freshly ground black pepper
4 cups water

In a heavy saucepan dry-roast the caraway seeds; now add the butter and sauté the onion until transparent; add celery and potatoes and cook, stirring frequently, for about ten minutes. Now add the water, and boil for a further fifteen minutes, adding the parsley just before serving. This is delicious garnished with some yoghurt or sour cream.

Chopped swede tops, cooked in a little water, are very good added to the above soup.

POTATO AND MISO SOUP

2 leeks, sliced, including the dark green
3 potatoes, scrubbed and diced
1 Tbs. dill seed
Pinch of thyme
4 cups water
2-3 Tbs. miso (to taste)
2 Tbs. butter
Salt, pepper

Melt butter in saucepan and add leeks; cook until they change colour then add the diced potatoes, salt, pepper, thyme and dill seeds. Cook a further ten minutes, stirring well. Finally add the softened miso and cook ten minutes or so more.

MAIN COURSES

Winter is the time for closing in on ourselves, and for quietness. It is also the natural season for eating bean and grain dishes. Of course, we eat these all year round, but during the winter months these dishes come into their own, with vegetables cooked along with or served with them, and with a selection of the preserved vegetables that have been put by to add a piquant flavour to the whole. Or served with grated salads which our family is very fond of.

I've subdivided this section into Beans, Fish, Groats, Potatoes, and Wheat (or Rye), because that's generally how I think about the main courses during this season. Recipes for vegetables available in this season (notably cabbage, broccoli, carrots and celery) will be found in the previous chapters.

Beans

All recipes are for tic beans because these are the beans that can be grown in Britain; however, other beans may be substituted either in whole or in part.

BASIC BAKED TIC BEANS

- 3 cups tic beans, soaked overnight
- 1 carrot, cut into strips (optional)
- 2 onions, quartered
- 1 bay leaf (optional)
- Pinch of thyme and rosemary (optional)
- ¼ cup olive oil
- Lemon juice
- Salt, black pepper

Combine beans, carrot, onions and seasoning with enough water to cover, and cook over a low heat for three hours. Drain, toss well in the olive oil, pour over the lemon juice, add salt and pepper if more is wanted, and put in a casserole to bake gently for an hour, adding a little of the cooking water if desired.

This is a good basic accompaniment for most dishes. The tic bean is the same as the ordinary brown bean which forms a basis for many Middle-Eastern diets.

BOSTON BAKED BEANS

- 3 cups tic beans, soaked overnight
- 4 rashers streaky bacon
- 1 rounded tsp. mustard powder
- 1 tsp. (or more to taste) salt
- 3 tsp. brown sugar
- 2 Tbs. treacle or molasses (the latter is far better to use)
- 1 cup boiling water

Cook beans until tender—about three hours. Cut up the bacon and cook slowly in a small saucepan to render the fat; add seasonings and molasses or treacle, stirring well, and mix in the boiling water. Place the beans in a casserole; pour over the molasses and bacon mixture; add more water to cover and bake in a low oven for about four hours. Add one chopped cooking apple and a pinch of ginger for a delightful difference.

Fish

Winter is the best season for cheap fish—or perhaps I should say cheaper fish. But below are three recipes for white fish.

INDIAN FISH OVER WHEAT IN CASSEROLE

2 cups white fish, boned
2 cups yoghurt
1 onion, finely chopped
Pinch ground cloves
2 tsp. turmeric
2 tsp. salt
2 tsp. ground coriander
½ tsp. anise
½ cup melted butter
3 cups pre-cooked wheat
salt, pepper

Combine the yoghurt, onion, and seasonings; marinade the fish in this mixture for at least an hour.

Take about two tablespoons of the butter and heat in a casserole; take out the fish from the marinade, and brown slightly in the casserole. Now add half the marinade and the rest of the butter; cover with the wheat and then pour over the remaining marinade. Add salt and pepper if you wish at this stage; cover the casserole and bake in a moderate oven (325°F) for about forty-five minutes.

CURRIED FISH OVER GROATS

2 cups white fish, boned
2 tsp. salt
1 tsp. turmeric
½ cup white wine vinegar (or Cider Vinegar, p. 00)
4 onions, chopped fine
4 cloves garlic, crushed
2 tsp. grated ginger root
Pinch of ground chili peppers
¾ cup oil
1 cup water

Marinade the fish in the vinegar mixed with the salt and turmeric and let stand at least an hour.

Mix thoroughly together the chopped onions, garlic, ginger root and chili peppers.

Heat oil in heavy skillet and add the onion mixture, stirring constantly for a few minutes; place drained fish in the skillet and add the cup of water. Stir to coat and mix and cook for about thirty minutes or until the fish flakes easily. If you want, a little of the vinegar marinade can be added.

Serve with plain boiled groats and any one of the many chutneys from the autumn section of the book.

FISH BALLS WITH MASH

2 cups boned white fish
1 tsp. salt
Grated black pepper
2 cloves garlic, crushed
4 Tbs. butter
3 Tbs. flour
Yoghurt
Oil for frying

Grind or chop the fish very fine and add the salt, pepper and garlic. Cream the butter and flour and work this mixture into the fish, softening with yoghurt as you go. Form into balls and fry the balls until brown on all sides.

Place the fish balls on top of mashed potatoes, sprinkle a little grated cheese on top and brown for a minute or two under the grill.

Herring

White fish is fine and good, but winter really is the season for herring for this is when our big herring catches are landed in the North and West of Scotland, particularly from boats working the Minches. To date these waters have not been over-fished and the herring come year after year—so heavy is the catch that exporting vessels taking a proportion straight to fishmarkets in Denmark are called 'klondikers' locally. Of course, this glut of herring will not last long—indeed, some fear that already this area is in danger of being over-exploited. But, still, it is a stirring sight in a heavy souwester to watch the fishing boats tied up, sometimes six at a time, alongside a klondiker like sheltering ducklings, while baskets of fish weave and bob through flying spume to the waiting holds below.

Not all the fish is exported of course, and some finishes up packed in barrels between alternate layers of salt for use eight to ten weeks later. Salt herring is a staple food in the diet of crofters and deserves to be sampled at least once by everyone. Ask your local fishmonger about suppliers if he doesn't stock them.

HERRING CASSEROLE

2 salt herrings
5 Tbs. butter
6 medium-sized raw potatoes
3 onions, sliced
1 Tbs. breadcrumbs
2 Tbs. dried dillweed or 1 Tbs. dill seed
Freshly ground black pepper

Clean herrings (remove heads), rinse well and soak in cold water overnight. Next morning cut along backbone, remove it and as many of the small bones as possible; pull off skin and drain the fillets on absorbent paper.

Melt half the butter in skillet; sauté onions until transparent. Scrub and thinly slice the potatoes.

Butter a shallow baking-dish and arrange, in alternate rows, the potatoes, onions, and herrings. Sprinkle with breadcrumbs and the seasoning and dot with remaining butter. Cover with aluminium foil and bake in a hot oven (425°F) for twenty-five or thirty minutes.

Delicious served with a shredded cabbage salad.

FRIED HERRING

4 salt herrings	1 egg, beaten
⅓ cup dry breadcrumbs	2 Tbs. yoghurt
¼ cup flour	4 Tbs. butter

Soak the herring and fillet as in the above recipe. Mix the breadcrumbs and flour together in a large plate. Mix together the beaten egg and yoghurt in shallow bowl. Dip the herring first in the breadcrumb mixture, then the egg, then again in the breadcrumbs, and fry in the butter.

Serve with whole boiled potatoes and a shredded cabbage salad.

HERRING WITH APPLE

4 salt herrings	1 cup sour cream (or yoghurt)
4 Tbs. butter	2 Tbs. breadcrumbs
2 onions, sliced	
4 slices stale bread	
1 large or 2 medium cooking apples	

Soak the herring overnight and fillet as for Herring Casserole, above. Melt butter in skillet and brown the onions. Coarsely chop the herring, apples and bread and combine with sour cream and onions. Turn into a buttered baking-dish and sprinkle with the breadcrumbs.

Bake in a medium-hot oven (400°F) for about thirty minutes. Serve hot with baked potatoes and a salad.

CHOPPED HERRING

This is a salad-type recipe which is delicious served with plain boiled potatoes.

4 salt herrings	3 Tbs. Cider Vinegar (p. 196)
1 onion, finely chopped	2 slices bread
1 cooking apple, chopped	

- 2 hard-boiled eggs
- 3-4 stalks celery, chopped
- Pinch of sugar
- 2 Tbs. salad oil

Soak and fillet the herrings as for Herring Casserole, p. 163.

Chop together the herring, the apple, onion, celery and eggs. Pour vinegar over the bread and add to the herring with the sugar and oil; chop until very smooth; taste for seasoning (more vinegar may be wanted) and chill before serving.

HERRING SALAD

This is another dish which is excellent served with plain boiled potatoes.

- 4 salt herrings
- 1 onion, chopped
- 2 red winter radishes, grated
- 1 black winter radish, grated
- 1 small celeriac, grated
- ¼ cup Cider Vinegar (p. 196)
- 4 Tbs. salad oil
- Pinch of sugar
- ½ tsp. paprika
- Freshly ground black pepper

Treat the herrings as for Herring Casserole (p. 163) and cut into bite-size pieces; toss together with the grated celeriac, onion and radishes. Pour over the oil, vinegar and seasoning and toss well; refrigerate before serving.

PICKLED HERRING

This is the last herring recipe, and our favourite. It will keep for about a week (and is better for the keeping) and should be served with plain boiled potatoes and lots of pickled cucumbers.

- 6 salt herrings
- 4 onions, sliced thin
- 1 cup Cider Vinegar (p. 196)
- ¼ cup water
- 1 tsp. sugar
- 2 tsp. mixed pickling spice
- 2 bay leaves
- 1 cup sour cream (or yoghurt)

Soak and fillet herrings as above. Cut into two-inch pieces and in a glass jar (or bowl) arrange the herrings and onions in alternate layers.

Boil together the vinegar, water, and seasoning for a few minutes; cool slightly and pour over the herring. Cover tightly and shake to make sure the vinegar water goes well down. Refrigerate for at least two days before serving.

Groats

BASIC SEASONED GROATS

To every two cups of well-drained cooked groats, add a good pinch of thyme, basil, salt and pepper. If you want the dish slightly more crispy, melt some butter in a skillet and pour the seasoned groats into it. Stirring constantly, cook until well buttered—about three minutes—over a medium heat.

GROATS WITH BRUSSEL SPROUTS

Wash and clean your Brussel sprouts, cutting larger ones in half; melt some butter in a saucepan and add the sprouts, seasoned with salt, pepper, and a good sprinkling of soya sauce. Mix thoroughly, cover and cook for about ten minutes or until they begin to change colour. Add equal amount of well-rinsed, cooked groats, and toss together in the saucepan, cooking only long enough to heat through. Serve either plain (with side dish of yoghurt and perhaps some pickled vegetables) or with a plain, cheese or mushroom sauce.

GROATS WITH KALE IN CASSEROLE

Curly kale is a wonderful vegetable, standing well throughout the winter months and even standing up to wind. And, when the larger leaves have been picked, smaller sprouts grow which, in the early spring when vegetables are scarce, are delicious served chopped raw in a salad.

However, for this recipe we use the larger leaves, and the stalks. Chop up your kale roughly, and place in saucepan with just enough water (or stock) to cover. Kale is a 'hard' vegetable and needs water to cook properly, but don't overcook it—about fifteen to twenty minutes is ample.

Butter a casserole dish and place a layer of kale, a layer of well-rinsed groats, a layer of kale, etc., and top with thinly-sliced rounds of onion. Pour over this a garlic sauce—or any sauce of your choosing—and bake in a moderate oven for about half an hour.

GROAT CAKES

1 cup rinsed cooked groats
1 cup wholewheat flour
½ tsp. salt
½—¾ cup water
¼ cup sesame seeds
Oil for frying

Mix together the groats, wheat, and salt with just enough water to form a workable mixture. Pat out on floured surface and knead slightly—pull off snippets and roll or pat these into rounds. Sprinkle sesame seeds on surface and press seeds into the cakes on both sides. Fry in oil until a golden brown.

Can be eaten hot like meat patties, with ketchup, pickled vegetables and a hearty dish, or with turnips and cabbage, or eaten cold for late night suppers.

GROAT LOAF

2 cups rinsed cooked groats
1 cup cooked dried peas
½ cup chopped walnuts
1 egg
1 tsp. salt
Black pepper
2 Tbs. melted butter
Milk for mixing

Put cooked peas through strainer to remove skins; now mix with the groats and other ingredients, using only just enough milk to form a stiffish consistency. Place in a greased loaf-tin and bake, covered with oiled paper, for about thirty minutes in a moderate oven (300°F).

Potatoes

POTATO LATKES

This is our favourite potato recipe—the cakes are crunchy and, of course, fattening.

1 lb. well-scrubbed potatoes
1 large onion
2-4 Tbs. wholewheat flour
Salt, freshly ground black pepper
Butter or oil for frying

Coarsely grate the potatoes into a large bowl; squeeze out as much of the water as possible. Grate in the onion, add salt and pepper, and add just enough flour so that the potatoes will hold together.

Put a good quantity of oil or butter into a heavy skillet, heat, and drop potato mixture by generous spoonfuls into pan. Level off with the back of a spoon so that you have a proper pancake shape. When they are sizzling around the edges, turning a golden brown, turn them. The oil or butter should be always hot around the latke (pancake), but not covering it.

They can be kept hot (and will crispen slightly) in a low oven while the rest are cooking. Serve hot with

chopped apple and nuts, or
apple sauce with cinnamon, or
yoghurt or sour cream, or
a combination of the sour cream and yoghurt with the apples

POTATOES WITH CARAWAY SEED

Boil well-scrubbed potatoes; drain (and save water for soups, sauces, etc.).

Put about two tablespoons of butter in heavy skillet, add one heaped tablespoon of caraway seeds and cook until they sizzle. Add cut-up potatoes, stirring well, and cook until they are brown. Sprinkle with salt and serve with Ground Meat (p. 44) and a salad.

CREAMED POTATOES

4 cups cooked cold potatoes, cubed
½ cup milk
1 tsp. salt
1 Tbs. dill seed
Black pepper
2 Tbs. butter
2 Tbs. chopped American cress or parsley

Put the potatoes with the milk into saucepan and cook over a low gentle heat until the potatoes have absorbed most of the milk; add butter and seasonings and cook for a further five minutes. Serve hot with an omelette and a salad.

POTATO KUGEL

3 eggs
3 cups grated, drained potatoes
¼ cup wholewheat flour
½ tsp. baking powder
2 tsp. salt
Black pepper, freshly ground
1 onion, thinly sliced
4 Tbs. melted butter or fat

Beat the eggs until thick and frothy; stir in the well-drained potatoes, the flour, baking powder, and the rest of the ingredients. Turn into a greased casserole and bake in a moderate oven for one hour. Serve either in the casserole, or turn out on a dish. This is equally good cold.

POTATO AND CARROT CHARLOTTE

1 cup grated carrots
3 cups grated, well-drained potatoes
3 egg yolks, beaten
4 cream crackers, crumbled
2 tsp. salt
Pinch of sugar
1 scant tsp. grated ginger root
4 Tbs. melted butter or fat
3 stiffly-beaten egg whites

Mix the potatoes, egg yolks, crackers, seasonings and the melted butter or fat. Add the carrots and about half a cup of water; stir well.

Fold the above mixture into the stiffly-beaten egg whites and put into a large greased casserole. Bake in a moderate oven for about an hour.

SPECIAL POTATO CURRY

5 medium-sized potatoes, scrubbed and diced
3 Tbs. butter
1 tsp. salt
1 tsp. cummin seeds
½ tsp. mustard seeds (or powder)
1 tbs. coriander seeds (or powder)
1 tsp. turmeric
1 tsp. grated ginger root
½ tsp. cayenne pepper
2 cups water
1 cup yoghurt
1 cup cooked, dried peas

Heat butter in heavy saucepan and add to it all the spices; let them simmer together three to four minutes, stirring frequently. Add potatoes and stir well to coat them; cook thus until the potatoes are golden and even a little crisp—about ten minutes. Now add the water and simmer the potatoes slowly for thirty minutes. Finally, add the yoghurt and peas and, stirring well, heat for five minutes or so. Serve with any of the chutneys from the Preserves section, pp. 141-4.

Wheat (or Rye)

BASIC HERBED WHEAT

Cook the wheat as directed in Chapter I, pp. 12-13. While it is still warm and excess cooking-water is evaporating, add crumbled rosemary, black pepper or any herbs you wish. Stir well and cover for five minutes before serving. Or, if a slightly crispy wheat is desired, turn it into a skillet in which some butter has been melted and, stirring constantly, cook until it is browned and the herbs are well blended.

WHEAT WITH LEEKS

3 cups cooked wheat
2-3 Tbs. butter

3-4 leeks
Good pinch of dried marjoram
Salt and black pepper

Melt butter in heavy skillet or pot; slice leeks and sauté until they turn a bright green; add marjoram, salt and finally the wheat; toss lightly to coat. Cook thus for about ten minutes, stirring every now and then to prevent sticking. Or, alternatively, once leeks have been sautéd, turn them and the remaining ingredients into a greased casserole and bake for about twenty minutes in a moderate oven (300–325°F).

WHEAT WITH JERUSALEM ARTICHOKES

3 cups cooked wheat
1 lb. (or more) Jerusalem artichokes, well scrubbed, and sliced
2 onions, sliced
1 Tbs. wholewheat flour
½ cup white wine
2 cloves garlic, crushed
Salt, black pepper
Grated nutmeg
2 Tbs. butter

Melt butter in saucepan and sauté onions; add flour and stir, cooking till onions are well browned. Add the wine and the artichokes, garlic and nutmeg; stir and cook for about five minutes.

Put wheat in a well-greased casserole; pour over the artichokes and cover with oiled paper. Bake for about twenty minutes in a moderate oven (300–325°F)—just long enough to heat the wheat and let the artichokes soften a bit.

WHEAT CASSEROLE

Mix wheat with beaten egg, grated onion, grated parsnip, grated carrot and cubed swedes. Season with salt, pepper, basil and garlic. Add just enough flour and milk or water so it will make a good loaf. Turn into a casserole and bake in a moderate oven (300–325°F) for thirty minutes. Pour over a sauce of your choice and bake a further thirty minutes.

WHEAT AND GROATS COMBINATION

Take equal amounts of pre-cooked groats and wheat and sauté with onion in a quantity of butter; sprinkle liberally with soya sauce and serve with any oriental-style vegetable dish.

CREAM OF WHEAT (BUT BEST MADE WITH RYE)

1 cup whole rye or wheat grains	1 cup shredded cabbage
2 Tbs. vegetable oil	1 Tbs. caraway seeds
1 onion, diced	Salt
	3 cups water, boiling

Roast rye (or wheat) in moderate oven until light brown (or dry-roast in skillet until light brown); crack in a grinder and sauté in a skillet in which oil has been heated; stir gently until it gives off a sweet aroma. Set aside.

In heavy pot put just enough oil to cover and heat; sauté onions until transparent; add cabbage and caraway seeds and cook until almost tender; add rye and salt, cover with the boiling water and cook until soft and thick. Excellent served in large flat bowls, with *Pidé* (pp. 211-12) and a selection of pickled vegetables. (See Preserves section, pp. 145-52).

SALADS

This is the season when grated salads come into their own; there is absolutely no restriction as to what vegetable goes with what, and it is best simply to experiment. However, below are some of our favourite combinations, including some for Sprouted Seeds (p. 219).

RED AND BLACK WINTER RADISHES

Grate equal quantities of the long black Spanish and the red (or rose) round winter radish; toss in as much American cress as you like (we usually like half as much as the radish) and pour over a Sesame Seed and Olive Oil Dressing (p. 198). Toss well before serving.

CHICORY

Slice the chicory lengthwise and arrange on a platter; place thin rounds of onion in a decorative pattern and, just before serving, pour over a basic olive oil and lemon dressing to which tarragon and a little garlic has been added.

CELERIAC, CARROT AND CRESS

Grate well-scrubbed celeriac, slice a quantity of carrots and add a good handful of chopped American cress. Toss in a vinaigrette dressing.

DANDELION

Dandelion can be forced like chicory. Gather the roots in the autumn and force in a pot, over which another pot has been placed to keep out the light. Treat as chicory, above.

JERUSALEM ARTICHOKES

Well scrub the artichokes and grate into a bowl; combine with a selection of pickled vegetables and toss well in a mayonnaise thinned with a little yoghurt.

TURKISH LEEK SALAD – 1

Boil some medium-sized leeks, drain (reserving water for soup or sauce), slice and squeeze on a little lemon juice. When cool, put a dash of olive oil over them, and salt and pepper, and serve.

TURKISH LEEK SALAD – 2

Boil leeks as above but, when cooling them, drain away most of the water, leaving just enough to cover them. Combine this water with a small amount of cornflour (about one scant teaspoon to half a cup of water) and return to the water, stirring only until it thickens. Continue stirring and squeeze in some lemon juice and olive oil—the sauce should be thick but transparent. Cool before serving.

PARSNIPS, CRESS AND ORANGE PEEL

Grate well-scrubbed parsnips into a bowl. Add the same amount of American cress (or winter spinach if it's nice) and grate in a little orange peel for piquancy. Pour over a simple vinaigrette.

POTATO SALAD

- 2 lb. potatoes—approx. the same size and not too large
- 2 onions
- 2 tsp. salt
- ½ tsp. freshly-ground black pepper
- ½ cup Mayonnaise (pp. 198-9)
- 2 Tbs. Cider Vinegar (p. 196)
- Bay leaf
- Optional:
  - Dill seed or weed
  - Garlic
  - Chopped chives

Scrub the potatoes and boil in salted water, to which a bay leaf has been added, just long enough to cook them; make sure they're still firm.

While warm, peel the potatoes and cube them. (Reserve both the cooking water and the peels—the latter can be chopped and added to the water for soups.) Grate onions into the potatoes, add seasoning. Combine the vinegar with the mayonnaise and pour over the potatoes. Can be served hot or cold.

WHEAT AND GROAT SALAD

1 cup cooked, well-rinsed groats
1 cup cooked, well-rinsed wheat
(or 2 cups of one of the grains)
½ cup American Cress, chopped
1 cup bean sprouts
3 Tbs. oil
1 Tbs. vinegar
1 Tbs. soya sauce

Combine the grains, cress and sprouts; mix together the oil, vinegar and the soya sauce and add to the grains. Toss well and chill for at least thirty minutes before serving to blend the flavours.

SPROUTS AND ROOTS

Take equal amounts of grated roots (parsnips, carrots or one of the winter radishes) and sprouted seeds. Toss in a toasted Seed Dressing (p. 198).

CHOPPED WINTER SPINACH

Chop winter spinach and place in bowl; add to this some sliced carrot, chopped hard-boiled egg, grated cheese and thin sticks of winter radish. Toss in a vinaigrette flavoured with garlic.

SWEDE AND CHEESE

If you are growing your own swedes, then this is a good recipe to try; if you're buying your swedes, it is essential to get a freshly dug swede for this.

Scrub the swede and peel. (The peels can be chopped and if boiled will make a good stock for soup or sauces.) Grate into bowl and add a good quantity of grated Cheddar cheese. Pour over a Mayonnaise Dressing (pp. 198-9).

DESSERTS

Since most of our winter main dishes are quite substantial, we finish many of our meals with apples and cheese. However, when I do make desserts, they tend to group themselves into one of the following categories: Apple, Oats, and Yeast.

Apple

BAKED APPLE WITH NUTS

Wash, core, and peel half-way down six medium-sized cooking apples. Pour over them a syrup made by boiling together one cup of brown sugar with one-and-a-half cups water for five minutes. Let the apples simmer, turning carefully, until they are tender. Remove from syrup and stick nuts (almonds are best) into the peeled half. Place in buttered baking dish, pour syrup over them, and bake in hot oven (400° F) just long enough to brown the nuts (about ten minutes). Can be served hot or cold and delicious, of course, with whipped cream.

APPLE BROWN BETTY

I don't know how this recipe (which is, basically, a scalloped apple recipe) got its name but it is our favourite apple dessert.

4 apples, cored and chopped (don't peel)
2 cups crushed cream crackers or water biscuits
½ cup brown sugar
1 lemon, juice and rind
½ tsp. cinnamon
½ tsp. grated nutmeg
2 Tbs. butter
¼ cup water

Melt the butter and add the crumbled biscuits; mix sugar and spices with grated lemon rind. Put a quarter of the crumbs in the bottom of a buttered baking dish; add half the apples and sprinkle with half the sugar and spices. Add another quarter of the crumbs, the rest of the apple and then the sugar and spices. Sprinkle lemon juice over all, top with the remainder of the crumbs, cover (with aluminium foil if no cover on dish) and bake in a moderate oven (325–350°F); uncover and put under the grill to brown quickly. Like all apple dishes, delicious served with cream.

APPLE CHARLOTTE, FANCY

5 cooking apples, grated
Some grated lemon rind
2 Tbs. red wine
4 Tbs. brown sugar
½ cup butter, melted
2 cups stale breadcrumbs (or a mixture of crumbled digestive biscuits and cream crackers)
4 Tbs. brown sugar
Crushed walnuts for garnish

Grate the apples and combine with the lemon rind, wine and sugar; cook gently for a few minutes to combine flavours. Combine melted butter, crumbs and the other four tablespoons of sugar and toast lightly.

In buttered baking dish place one-third of the crumbs, then half the apples, then another third of the crumbs, the remaining apples and finally the remaining crumbs. Press mixture down firmly, garnish with nuts, chill and serve cold.

DUTCH APPLE CAKE

4 cooking apples
2 Tbs. sugar mixed with cinnamon and grated nutmeg
2 cups flour
3 tsp. baking powder
½ tsp. salt
3 Tbs. butter
1 egg, beaten
⅔ cup (approx.) milk

Mix and sift the dry ingredients; work in the butter with finger tips (or a blender if you're squeamish); add the milk with the well-beaten egg and mix quickly with a knife. Dough must be soft enough to spread; over-mixing will just make it rather tough.

Spread the dough in a well-buttered shallow baking dish; press into it the apples which have been cored, cut in quarters, then sliced in half again. Traditionally the apples are placed in rows, lengthwise; sprinkle the apples with the sugar mixture and bake in a hot oven (400° F) for about thirty minutes. Good served hot with Lemon Sauce (pp. 201-2).

APPLE DUMPLINGS

This is a great favourite with children.

1 Biscuit Dough (as for Strawberry Shortcake, p. 102)	6 cooking apples, cored
	1 cup brown sugar
	1 cup water

Make your biscuit dough and roll out into six, six-inch squares. Place on each an apple and one tablespoon of sugar, bring up the corners, twist and pinch together on top, and place in a well-greased pan. Pour over the six dumplings the water and the remaining sugar and bake in a hot oven (400° F) for forty-five minutes or until crisp and nicely brown.

APPLE FRITTERS

For the batter you will need:

1 egg, separated	½ cup flour
¼ cup water or milk	1 Tbs. butter
Pinch of salt	

To the beaten yolk add the butter and salt and half of the liquid; stir in the flour to make a smooth paste. Add remainder of liquid gradually to make the batter, and finally fold in the stiffly-beaten egg white.

Core and slice two or three cooking apples. Dip pieces in batter and fry quickly in deep hot fat; serve sprinkled with icing sugar and lemon slices on the side.

If you want a bit of exotica, try using bananas or slices of pineapple: that would be an authentic finish to an oriental meal.

APPLE MUFFINS

½ cup brown sugar
1 egg
2 cups sifted flour
Pinch of salt
3 tsp. baking powder
1 tsp. cinnamon
1 cup milk
¼ cup melted butter
2 cups apples, chopped fine

Mix together the sugar and egg, beating well with a wooden spoon; sift together the flour, baking powder, salt and cinnamon; add to sugar and egg mixture, add milk, butter and apples and blend thoroughly.

Fill greased muffin tins three-quarters full and bake in a hot oven (400°F) for about twenty-five minutes.

Delicious served hot, split open and spread with butter, alongside a dish of Spiced Apple Sauce (below).

APPLE PIE

Follow directions for fruit pies in the Summer section (pp. 206-8) substituting apples mixed with either walnuts or hazelnuts for the fruit given.

SPICED APPLE SAUCE

For every pound of cooking apples used, use half a cup strong left-over herbal tea, a quarter cup brown sugar, some stick cinnamon, two whole cloves and two to three whole allspice. Cook together until soft then press through sieve or strainer. Cool and serve.

APPLE SAUCE CAKE

½ cup butter
1 cup brown sugar
1 egg, well beaten
1 cup dates, chopped fine
1½ cups Apple Sauce (above)
1 cup hazelnuts or walnuts, chopped coarse
1 cup sultanas
1 tsp. cinnamon
½ tsp. grated nutmeg
1 tsp. vanilla
2 cups flour
2 tsp. soda

Cream together the butter and sugar; add egg and vanilla. Combine all the dry ingredients and mix with above mixture. Finally, add the rest of the ingredients, turn into well buttered loaf pan and bake in a moderate oven (350° F) for an hour.

Oats

OAT CRUNCH

½ cup each of
  brown flour
  porridge oats
  dessicated coconut
  brown sugar
  butter
1 egg
1 tsp. baking powder
Pinch of salt
2 Tbs. honey dissolved in 2 Tbs. hot water

Cream together the butter and sugar; add egg and the rest of the ingredients, mixing together well. Drop by spoonfuls onto greased baking sheet; flatten with wetted spoon and bake in moderate oven (275–300° F) for about fifteen minutes.

OATMEAL COOKIES

½ cup butter
½ cup brown sugar
1 egg, well beaten
1 cup flour
1 cup oatmeal
2 Tbs. milk
Scant tsp. baking powder
Pinch of soda
Pinch of salt
1 tsp. cinnamon
½ cup chopped dates, raisins or sultanas
½ cup chopped walnuts or hazelnuts

Cream together butter and sugar; add egg. Mix together rest of the dry ingredients, sprinkle over raisins and nuts and combine mixtures, adding just enough milk to make a stiff dough.

Drop on greased baking sheet one inch apart and bake in oven at 350°F for ten to fifteen minutes.

LACY OAT COOKIES

2½ cups porridge oats
1 cup brown sugar
½ cup melted butter
2 tsp. baking powder
1 egg, beaten

Add melted butter to dry ingredients; add beaten egg and mix well. Drop from spoon onto greased baking sheets and bake for eight to ten minutes at 350°F. Let stand a minute or so before removing from sheet.

MACROBIOTIC OAT COOKIES

3 cups porridge oats
½ cup currants
1½ cups strong herbal tea
Pinch of salt
1 tsp. coriander, ground
½ tsp. vanilla
3 Tbs. oil
¼ cup roasted sesame or sunflower seeds

Boil the currants in the tea for a couple of minutes and let stand while you dry-roast the oats over a high flame (using a dry skillet), stirring constantly, until the oats smell very sweet.

Place oats in bowl and add the rest of the dry ingredients; combine the oil with the currants, mix, and add to the oats, mixing it well. Let this batter stand for fifteen minutes. Lightly grease a baking sheet; drop batter onto it by spoonfuls and cook in a moderately hot oven (375°F) for about ten minutes.

OAT SHORTBREAD

2 cups porridge oats
2 cups self-raising flour
½ cup brown sugar
1 cup butter
Pinch of salt

Cream the butter and sugar together; work in the oats, flour and salt quickly. Do not knead the dough. Press into round cake tins and bake in a moderately low oven (250–275°F) for about forty-five minutes or more.

STEAMED OAT AND DATE PUDDING

1 cup porridge oats
½ lb. chopped dates
2 eggs
½ cup molasses (or treacle will do)
⅔ cup water
½ tsp. soda
Pinch of salt
Juice of half a lemon

Thoroughly mix all the ingredients and steam in a well-greased pudding dish for about three hours. Serve with any sweet sauce.

Yeast

DANISH PASTRY

¾ pt. milk, scalded (less if egg is used)
¾ cup butter
¾ cup brown sugar
1 tsp. salt
6 cups flour (approx.)
1 oz. yeast
1 egg
Grated rind of half a lemon

Crumble yeast in cup with a teaspoon of the sugar and half a cup of the scalded milk cooled to blood temperature. (Test milk on inside of your wrist: if the milk feels hot, wait a bit; if the milk feels cold, you've waited too long and so must heat the milk a little! The idea is to not feel the milk.) Let yeast stand in a warm place as you continue with the dough. Pour scalded milk into deep basin; add butter, lemon rind, the rest of the sugar and the salt. When cooled to lukewarm add the beaten egg and finally stir in the yeast mixture and half of the flour. Now add more flour but take care not to add too much; just enough so you can knead the dough until it is very smooth and elastic. Cover with damp tea towel and let rise in warm place until double in bulk—about one to two hours—during which time you can prepare the filling.

1½ cups finely chopped apple
½ cup coarsely ground nuts
¼ cup mixed dried fruit
1 tsp. cinnamon
½ tsp. cardamon seed, crushed
4 Tbs. melted butter
½ cup brown sugar

Place all the ingredients except the melted butter in a bowl and mix thoroughly. Pour over the butter and mix again. Set aside until dough is ready.

When dough has risen, punch down and put onto floured surface. Roll out to about half-inch thickness and cut into six-inch squares. Place a dollop of the filling onto each square, and fold into a triangle, pressing edges together with a floured fork. Place triangles on greased baking sheet and bake, without proofing, in moderate oven (325—350°F) for twenty to thirty minutes. When cool, they can be dusted with icing sugar or glazed with a simple clear icing.

DRESDEN FRUIT BREAD

2 oz. active dry yeast
¼ cup warm water
¾ cup milk
1 cup butter
4 cups flour
2 eggs
½ cup sugar
½ tsp. salt
¾ cup chopped raisins
½ cup coarsely chopped almonds
¼ cup mixed peel
Grated rind of 1 lemon

Sprinkle yeast over warm water to soften; heat milk and butter together and cool to lukewarm. In a large bowl put two cups of flour and make a well in the centre; place milk, yeast mixture, unbeaten eggs, sugar and salt in the well and mix thoroughly a few minutes. (This can be done in an electric mixer using medium speed.) Reserving about a quarter-cup of the flour, add remaining flour to the dough and mix again, beating well with a wooden spoon if not using a mixer. Chill this thinnish dough overnight.

Punch dough down and mix slightly; cover with damp tea towel and set in warm place to rise until doubled; punch down again and again let it rise, but only until just about double.

Mix with the remaining quarter-cup flour the raisins, peel, nuts and lemon rind and knead this into the dough on a lightly floured surface.

Divide dough in half and pat each section into an oval about eight inches long; brush tops with a little melted butter and fold ovals in half, lengthwise,. Brush with more melted butter and place on greased baking sheet; let rise in warm place until double—about thirty minutes. Bake in moderate oven (375°F) for thirty to forty minutes, or until it sounds hollow when tapped with your knuckles. Remove from oven and brush with melted butter and sprinkle with a little icing sugar.

DOUGHNUTS

2 scant cups flour
½ cup brown sugar
1 oz. active dry yeast
½ cup warm milk
2 Tbs. butter, melted
1 egg
Pinch of salt
½ tsp. cinnamon
1 tsp. grated nutmeg
nutmeg

Dissolve yeast in the warm milk with the melted butter, and one teaspoon of the sugar. Beat egg, sugar, salt and spices with a whisk; when the yeast is dissolved and bubbly, combine the two mixtures, whisking to keep it frothy.

Now add the flour with a wooden spoon—just enough to make a soft, smooth dough. Cover with a damp tea towel and let rise for about an hour. Punch down and turn out onto lightly floured surface; knead until soft and elastic, adding more flour if necessary.

Now roll out about half an inch thick and cut with doughnut cutters or into small rounds (remember that the doughnuts puff up considerably). Leave to rest for fifteen minutes while you heat your oil to about

360–375°F (or until a cube of bread will brown in one minute).

Drop in the doughnuts, a few at a time; they should come up to the surface quickly, brown on one side, be turned, and brown on the other side. Drain on newspaper and, when cool, dust with sugar and cinnamon.

WALNUT ROLL

½ of dough as for Danish Pastry (pp. 182-3)
2 cups grated walnuts
¼ cup brown sugar
¼ cup honey

When the dough has risen, roll out to half-inch thickness and spread with the walnuts, sugar and honey, mixed to a thick paste. Roll into a long roll and form into a circle on a well-greased cake tin. Now, with a knife cut three-quarters the way through at regular intervals on the outside of the roll. Slightly turn the cut wedges to form a flower shape. Cover with a damp towel and let rise to double in bulk. Bake in moderate oven (350°F) until thoroughly done—start testing after about forty-five minutes. When cool, pour over a simple glaze of icing sugar and lemon juice.

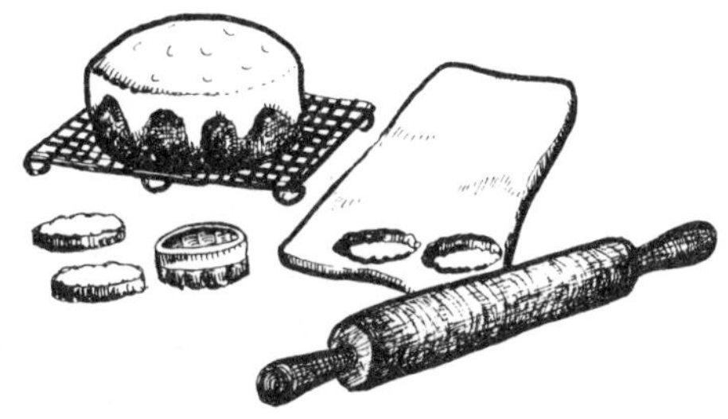

FESTIVE FARE

Festive fare generally means Christmas, and Christmas means, for most, turkey. But turkey is a dry, uninteresting-tasting bird and, ecologically, wasteful. Goose, that other traditional bird, might be exquisitely tasty but ecologically it also is wasteful; pounds of grain are consumed by these hungry birds in the winter and there are many who force-feed them grain to fatten them up for the market before Christmas.

But what about duck? Not the white Aylesbury duck (the one immortalized by Beatrix Potter) which doesn't lay eggs to any great degree and is not very good at foraging for its own food, but the brown khaki Campbell—a beautiful bird who lays lovely large blue-grey eggs which are excellent for baking (not good for whipping however) and who forages about for her food in both field and stream.

For this season our special menu would read thus:

Roast Glazed and Stuffed Duck
Spiced Tangerines
Baked Potatoes in their Jackets Brussels Sprouts Mayonnaise
Aged Fruit Cake

ROAST GLAZED AND STUFFED DUCK

1 5lb. (approx.) duck, drawn
2 tsp. salt and black pepper, mixed

Singe the duck to remove the pin feathers; wash, dry, and rub all over with the salt and pepper.

Remove as much of the fat from the cavity as possible (save fat and render, as for Chicken, pp. 45-6) and stuff with the following mixture, well combined:

2 cored, diced, cooking apples
10 stoned prunes, chopped
1 onion, grated
1 egg
4 Tbs. dry breadcrumbs

Sew up cavity and place on a rack in shallow baking pan; roast in hot oven (400°F) for thirty minutes; pour off fat and baste with the following honey mixture:

¼ cup honey
1 Tbs. soya sauce
2 Tbs. Cider Vinegar (p. 196)

Reduce heat to 350°F and roast a further two-and-a-half hours, basting with the honey mixture every half-hour. For the last basting, pour two tablespoons of sherry over the duck, then baste again.

To serve, snip the threads, letting stuffing and juice escape.

BAKED POTATOES IN THEIR JACKETS

Take your potatoes, of uniform size, and scrub well. Prick with a fork a few times and place in the oven on a rack above the duck about one-and-a-half hours or less (depending on size of potatoes) before the duck is to be served.

BRUSSELS SPROUTS MAYONNAISE

1 lb. Brussels sprouts—nice firm little heads
2 carrots, well scrubbed
2 parsnips, well scrubbed
2 Tbs. lemon juice
4 Tbs. Mayonnaise (pp. 198-9)
3-4 stalks celery, chopped

Combine all the vegetables, grating coarsely the Brussels sprouts; mix together the lemon juice with the mayonnaise, pour over the vegetables and toss well before serving.

SPICED TANGERINES

This dish must be made a few weeks in advance—as soon as the first firm tangerines hit the market. This is, by the way, the only recipe in this book which uses an imported food as a basis. However, seeing it's Christmas. . .

8 firm tangerines, well scrubbed
Whole cloves
2 cups dark brown sugar
1 cup Cider Vinegar (p. 196)
Some pieces of broken cinnamon sticks
1 tsp. anise seeds

Stick a small quantity of whole cloves into each tangerine—about six or eight. Place carefully in an enamel saucepan. Bring to the boil the other spices, sugar and vinegar; pour over the tangerines and simmer gently for about ten to fifteen minutes. Place the fruit in hot clean jars, pour over the vinegar mixture to cover the fruit (add more vinegar if necessary), seal when cool and keep until needed.

To serve, place one for each person; to eat, simply slice and eat the fruit along with the duck.

AGED FRUIT CAKE

This also must be made well in advance. In fact, I make about three times the quantity below, in October, baking the cakes in loaf tins, clean coffee tins, reserving one enormous round cake tin for ourselves. The others, once baked, are wrapped in aluminium foil, then brown paper, and sent off to relatives in Australia and the States where they arrive, well aged, in time for Christmas or Chanukah.

- 1 lb. mixed peel and cherries
- 1 cup broken walnuts
- 1 cup raisins, chopped, or sultanas
- 1 cup currants
- ½ cup fruit juice
- ¼ cup molasses (or treacle)
- ¼ cup sherry or brandy
- 1 rounded tsp. each cinnamon grated nutmeg ground allspice
- ½ tsp. each salt and mace
- ¼ tsp. soda
- ½ cup butter
- 1 cup brown sugar
- 2 small cups flour
- 3 eggs

Combine peel, fruit, juice, molasses, spices and sherry or brandy in a large bowl and let stand overnight.

Prepare batter as follows:

Sift together salt, flour, soda and put aside. Cream butter and sugar until fluffy; beat in eggs one at a time, finally stir in flour and then fold in the fruit mixture.

Pack cake mixture firmly into two loaf tins which

have been well greased and lined with heavy brown oiled paper. Bake in slow, pre-heated oven (300°F) for about one-and-three-quarter hours. Remove loaves from tins and let cool; wrap well in aluminium foil and store in cool place for two months or so.

This is also the season for baking and so I will include our favourite cookie recipes—ones that we make only at this time of year and then hang from the Christmas tree lit by candles. For hanging, thread some sewing cotton through the cookies while they're still warm.

ALMOND PRETZELS

1 cup butter
1 cup sugar
½ lb. ground almonds
2 cups flour
2 yolks and 2 whole eggs (reserve extra egg whites for 'kisses', p. 191)

Cream butter and sugar, add eggs, almonds and the rest of the ingredients, beating well after each addition.

Mix and knead into one roll and let stand for a few hours in the fridge or a cool place to harden.

Now, pinch off pieces the size of a walnut and roll into pencil shape, twisting into a pretzel or whatever shape you like—we make plain circles, which look lovely when baked and hung from the tree. (Also, just the handy size and shape for small fingers to slip off the tree unnoticed.)

Place on greased baking sheet and bake in moderate oven (325—350°F) for about ten minutes, or until lightly brown.

ANISE COOKIES

3 eggs
1 cup sugar
1½—2 cups flour
1 Tbs. anise seed, well crushed
1 scant tsp. baking powder

Beat eggs very lightly, add sugar and continue beating—by hand for about thirty minutes(!) or with an electric mixer at medium speed for ten minutes. Add flour, sifted with the baking powder and the crushed anise seed. Beat for a further five minutes.

Drop by teaspoonfuls onto well greased and floured baking sheets, one inch apart. Let stand overnight at room temperature—a thin skin will have formed.

Bake in a moderate oven (350° F) for about twelve minutes—until a pale golden brown.

SPICED CHRISTMAS COOKIES

2 cups brown sugar
½ cup honey
¼ cup butter
1 tsp. cinnamon
½ tsp. mace
½ tsp. nutmeg
1 tsp. freshly-ground black pepper
2-2½ cups flour
1 Tbs. baking powder
1 egg
Juice and grated rind of ½ lemon
2 Tbs. milk

Add sugar to honey and cook until sugar is dissolved; add butter, mix, and cool. Add spices and flour, mixing in just enough flour so as to be able to handle the dough. Roll out thinly (⅛″) and cut with fancy shapes. Bake in greased baking sheets in moderate oven (350° F), for about ten minutes. When cool can be glazed with thin icing.

SOFT MOLASSES COOKIES

¾ cup butter
1 cup brown sugar
1 egg
1 cup molasses
1 tsp. soda
¾ cup hot water
4 cups flour
1 tsp. cinnamon
1 tsp. grated ginger root
Pinch of salt

Cream butter, add sugar, well-beaten egg, molasses and hot water; add the mixed and sifted dry ingredients. Drop by spoon onto greased baking sheets and bake for eight minutes in moderate oven (350° F). These cookies are not suitable for hanging made this way. But, if you want to hang them from a tree, chill the dough which has been rolled into a long sausage. Slice and bake as above.

SOUR MILK COOKIES

¼ cup butter
2 cups sugar
2 eggs
4 cups flour
1 cup sour milk or milk soured with 1 tsp. vinegar
1 tsp. soda

Cream butter and sugar; add eggs and mix well; add rest of ingredients, adding the soda to the soured milk before combining into dough. toss onto well floured surface, roll out very thinly and sprinkle with sugar (pressing sugar in lightly with rolling pin). Cut into shapes and bake on greased sheets in moderately hot oven (375°F) for about eight minutes.

KISSES

2 egg whites, very cold and fresh
½ cup caster sugar

Beat egg whites until very stiff but still shiny; add sugar, a couple of tablespoons at a time, beating all the while with wire whisk. Drop by teaspoonfuls onto well greased and floured baking sheets and bake in a very low oven (250°F) for about an hour. Or, these can even be done in a hot airing closet. Just pop the sheets by the water tank (on tops of the tank if possible) and leave until done. I've put them in in the morning, and we've eaten them in the evening.

But it is the day *after* all that festive fare that one wonders what possibly could be put on the table. If there's no left-over duck (as there never is with us) how about a selection of the following cold, buffet-style dishes, all of which can be prepared in advance, and are very good served with *Pidé* (which also can be made in advance, see pp. 211-12).

HUMUS

This is a Turkish (and Arab) dish made with equal amounts of puréed cooked chickpeas, tahina, and olive oil—seasoned with garlic, mint and lemon juice.

However, instead of chickpeas, I have made something resembling humus using puréed cooked dried peas in place of the chickpeas. Beat all the ingredients very well together; thin down with a little cold water so that the mixture is like thick mayonnaise. Pour into shallow bowl, garnish with lemon wedges, and let everyone simply dip in their *Pidé*.

MARINATED SMOKED SALMON WITH SOUR CREAM

If you were able to smoke your own salmon (pp. 94-5) it should be ready in time for Christmas. It is delicious served sliced thin, with piles of thinly sliced buttered Dark Bread (p. 209). But my favourite way of having smoked salmon is marinaded—a dish I've only ever had in New York.

- 12 slices smoked salmon, rolled into rollups
- 1 cup wine vinegar—white
- ¼ cup water
- 2 tsp. salt
- 1 bay leaf
- 4 cloves garlic, slivered
- 2 onions, sliced
- 1 small tsp. black peppercorns

Boil the vinegar, water, and spices and simmer for about two minutes. Arrange, in a clean glass jar, the smoked salmon and the onions; pour over the vinegar, cover and refrigerate for two to three days before serving with sour cream.

STUFFED VINELEAVES (DOLMA)

Preserved vineleaves, ready for stuffing, can be bought in many delicatessen shops. However, since grapes can now be grown in the south of the country, and are grown in conservatories in many houses, I thought I might include this very simple recipe for preparing your own vineleaves.

When living in southern France, near a convenient vineyard, I was surprised to learn that the peasants never preserved the vineleaves. But the very understandable reason was that, during World War II, they had their fill of vineleaves! Not having any recipe books handy, I thought of trying my hand at preserving a small bunch. It was quite easy and the result was very authentic.

Simply collect fresh green leaves; salt them well and stack them in a stone crock; cover with a brine solution (half a cup salt to two cups water) which has been boiled up with some cloves of garlic and then cooled down. Pour over the vineleaves, weigh the leaves down and leave for about two months or so. If you collect your leaves in early autumn or late summer, they will be ready for use at Christmas time.

Prepare the following stuffing:

- 1 cup cooked wheat (or groats)
- 1 small onion, grated or chopped fine
- 3 Tbs. small currants
- 1 tsp. dried dillweed (optional)
- 1 tsp. dried mint
- Enough olive oil to moisten mixture

Mix the above ingredients together very well—add less of the seasonings to suit your own taste. The above mixture is about enough for twelve to eighteen vineleaves.

Rinse the leaves in cold water and drain. Now, lay one out flat, put a spoonful of the mixture on the bottom end, and roll up, tucking the sides in well. When finished, place in the palm of your hand and give a good squeeze—this keeps the leaf from unfolding. Stack the finished stuffed leaves in a shallow pan. When all are done, squeeze over some lemon juice and pour about one cup of water mixed with one tablespoon of tomato purée over the leaves. Weigh down with a plate and cook over a gentle heat for about thirty to forty-five minutes. Eat cold, sprinkled with a little olive oil and lemon.

If you want to eat them hot, then, traditionally, they are made with a mixture of ground mutton and rice. In the above recipe, substitute half a cup minced mutton and half a cup cooked groats or wheat for the one cup of cooked grain; omit the mint and add more dill and a little garlic.

TARAMÁ

This is a very popular cod's roe *mézé* sold in Greece but a very good taramá can be made from local cod's roe, smoked and salted and available from many fishmongers or in jars.

To every half-cup of clean cod's roe, pound in a clove of garlic, the juice of half a lemon (or less) and about two tablespoons of olive oil and cold water, added alternately. Beat until the consistency is of a thick purée, adding more oil and/or water to taste. Pour into a shallow bowl and let everyone dip their *Pide* in and scoop out some.

TEA
BREAD
MUS
THE
MEDICINE

Chapter Six
Miscellanea

SALAD DRESSINGS

Basically, salad dressings are made by a proportion of oil and vinegar, perhaps with mayonnaise, and herbs, mixed thoroughly. It is important to use good ingredients if you want a good dressing—either olive or corn oil and cider or one of the vinegars given below.

FRUIT VINEGAR

Put cores and peelings of apples along with any other ripe but not spoiled fruit into a wide-mouthed stone crock. Make sure everything that goes into the crock has been well washed. Cover with cold water and keep in a warm place (an airing cupboard is ideal). More fruit can be added from time to time. A scum will form which will gradually thicken—this is the mother, or vinegar plant. From time to time taste the vinegar and, when it tastes strong enough, strain through a colander, then through cheese cloth, finally bottling and sealing up.

CIDER VINEGAR

Let sweet cider stand in an open jug (admitting the vinegar fly) from four to six weeks in a warmish place, by which time it will have turned to vinegar.

WINE VINEGAR

Treat red or white wine as for 'cider vinegar' above.

TARRAGON VINEGAR

Mix equal amounts of white wine and cider vinegar; in a bottle place two tarragon stalks and pour mixed vinegar into bottle; cover and let stand in the sun for three weeks before using.

BASIC HERB VINEGAR

Mix equal amounts of red and cider vinegar; crush into this some garlic, grate in some black pepper, a pinch of dried thyme and place in some fresh celery leaves. Cork and put away in a dark cupboard for three weeks.

Now, with oil and vinegar and a few herbs, it is possible to make a great variety of dressings, and they can be made in large quantities and kept in a corked bottle, shaken well before use.

BASIC VINAIGRETTE DRESSING OR FRENCH DRESSING

¼ cup vinegar
¾ cup olive (or corn) oil
1 Tbs. lemon juice
½ tsp. mustard powder
Salt, freshly ground black pepper

Mix together the lemon, vinegar and spices; add the olive oil, a little at a time, whisking well with a wire whisk so that the dressing is creamy. It can now be stored and shaken thoroughly before use.

GARLIC DRESSING

Add to the basic vinaigrette 1 clove garlic, crushed
1 Tbs. grated onion
1 tsp. pickled nasturtium seeds, chopped

Blend well and store as for basic Vinaigrette recipe, above.

STILTON CHEESE DRESSING

For every half cup of simple Vinaigrette, use one tablespoon of Stilton cheese. Mash the cheese with a fork and soften with the dressing, adding it a little at a time until all has been absorbed by the cheese.

TURKISH-STYLE DRESSING

Add to the basic vinaigrette 1 tsp. cummin, ground;
1 tsp. mint, well crushed

Combine thoroughly before using.

TOASTED SEED DRESSING

Take equal amounts of sea salt and sesame seeds (or sunflower, or pumpkin seeds) and dry-roast until they pop.

Add to one part of herb vinegar to three parts of olive oil.

YOGHURT DRESSING

1 cup yoghurt
2 Tbs. lemon juice
2 Tbs. Cider or White Wine Vinegar (p. 196)
Pinch of sugar
1 tsp. salt
Some black pepper, freshly ground
1 teaspoon prepared Mustard (below)

Whisk yoghurt until light and smooth; mix together all the other ingredients and add gradually to the yoghurt, whisking all the time. Will keep a few days.

MAYONNAISE

1 whole egg (not a duck egg)
1 tsp. mustard powder
1 tsp. salt
Pinch of sugar
1 cup oil (or more—add enough to make thick sauce)
1 Tbs. lemon juice
2 Tbs. tarragon vinegar

All ingredients, bowl and whisk should be cold before starting; put dry ingredients into bowl, add egg, and whisk until thick. Now start pouring in the oil, a few drops at a time to begin with, whisking constantly, then adding oil in a steady stream; alternate with some of the vinegar, beating after each addition until mixture is well blended and thick; end with the lemon juice.

Freshly chopped parsley, dill, chives, pickled vegetables, can be added to this very basic mayonnaise which will keep well in the fridge or any cool place.

MUSTARD

2 Tbs. each of melted
- butter
- mustard powder

1 Tbs. of ground cummin
1 tsp. salt
½ tsp. brown sugar
Tarragon or White Wine or Cider Vinegar (p. 196)

Mix the dry ingredients into the melted butter; add vinegar to make a creamy purée. Bottle in small jars, for it will keep well.

SAUCES

Savoury Sauces

BASIC BÉCHAMEL OR BROWN SAUCE

2 Tbs. butter
2 Tbs. brown flour
1 small onion, chopped fine
Pinch of thyme
Small bay leaf
2 cups hot milk or stock
Salt

Melt butter until bubbly; stir in the onions and cook until transparent; stir in the flour, mixing well and then the milk or stock, stirring constantly (use a wooden spoon). Add the herbs and salt and let cook slowly for about ten minutes so it will thicken.

BASIC BÉCHAMEL OR WHITE SAUCE

Follow the directions for sauce above, using white flour instead of brown, and making it with milk and not stock.

CHEESE SAUCE

Add half a teaspoon prepared mustard and half a cup of grated cheese to the basic white sauce; for a delicious difference, try making the sauce with half milk and half beer or stout.

YOGHURT SAUCE

Make the basic white sauce with half milk and half yoghurt, grating in a lot of black pepper and squeezing in a bit of lemon juice.

MISO SAUCE

To the basic brown sauce add one tablespoon of miso, softened with some of the sauce, and gently heated into the sauce with about one tablespoon of chopped parsley and celery leaves.

NASTURTIUM SAUCE

Add a quarter-cup drained and chopped Pickled Nasturtium Seeds (see p. 150) to basic Brown Sauce (see p. 199).

MUSHROOM SAUCE

Take one cup of chopped fresh mushrooms (Boletus Edulus—see p. 113—is really excellent for this) and sauté in two tablespoons of butter along with one small onion. Cover with about two cups of water and simmer with the cover on for about thirty minutes. Now proceed as for brown sauce above, using mushroom water in place of stock. Grate in some nutmeg before using, and stir in a tablespoon of sherry.

GARLIC SAUCE

Make a white sauce using half a cup of white wine in place of half a cup of the milk, adding the wine just at the end and only just heating the sauce through. Crush into sauce one or two cloves of garlic and add some powdered rosemary and tarragon.

HOLLANDAISE SAUCE

3 egg yolks
Pinch of salt
½ cup butter
1 Tbs. lemon juice
Dash of cayenne pepper

Beat the egg yolks until they are smooth and creamy; add salt and beat a further few minutes. Very gently melt the butter—it should not bubble—and now add it, drop by drop, to the egg yolk, mixing constantly; alternate with the lemon juice, also drop by drop, and beat constantly. Season with the cayenne pepper.

The sauce can be stored in the fridge for a day or so without danger of curdling and, incidentally, can be served cold with cooked vegetables or eggs. To serve hot, gently heat in top of double boiler (or on cool part of kitchen range), whisk well and serve immediately.

TOMATO SAUCE

8 tomatoes, skinned and chopped
1 onion, chopped
2-3 cloves garlic, chopped
1 bay leaf
2-3 Tbs. olive oil
1 tsp. dried tarragon (or 1 Tbs. chopped fresh)
Salt, pepper
1 cup (approx.) white wine

In a heavy skillet sauté onions in olive oil, with salt and pepper and the bay leaf, for a few minutes; add the chopped tomatoes, and the tarragon, and let this mixture cook, stirring a little to prevent sticking. When it has turned very soft, add your wine and simmer for about thirty minutes. Add more liquid as necessary.

This sauce can be stored in fridge and is excellent for pasta dishes.

Sweet Sauces

LEMON SAUCE

1 cup hot water
½ cup honey
4 Tbs. brown sugar
1 lemon, juice and peel
1 Tbs. cornflour
1 Tbs. butter

Mix sugar and cornflour; add water to honey and mix thoroughly; add water and honey mixture to sugar and cornflour gradually, stirring constantly. Cook for about ten minutes and finally add lemon juice, the grated peel and the butter. Mix and serve hot.

JAM SAUCE

Heat a quarter-cup jam (or marmalade), with the juice of a lemon and one-and-a-half cups of water. Stir well until dissolved and serve either hot or cold.

HARD SAUCE

¼ cup butter
1 cup icing sugar
½ tsp. rum, brandy or 1 tsp. vanilla

Cream the butter, add sugar gradually, and last add the flavouring. It is excellent served over hot apple desserts.

WINE SAUCE

1 cup brown sugar
⅓ cup water
1 tsp. vanilla
3 Tbs. brandy or red wine
1 Tbs. butter

Cook together the sugar and water for about five minutes—until it is a thick syrup. Remove from heat and add remaining ingredients.

BRANDY SAUCE

3 eggs, separated
Some icing sugar
1 Tbs. of brandy
A little grated orange peel

Beat egg yolks with enough sugar to sweeten, until thick and creamy; add brandy and then the stiffly-beaten egg whites; grate a little orange rind on top.

SOUP GARNISHES

CARAWAY POTATO STRIPS

1 cup mashed potatoes
½ cup butter
1 rounded cup flour
1 Tbs. caraway seed
Sea salt
1 egg, slightly beaten

Combine potatoes, butter, the flour and caraway seeds, mixing well with a fork; chill for thirty minutes.

Roll out on lightly floured surface; place on oiled baking sheet, brush with beaten egg and sprinkle liberally with sea salt and more caraway seeds. Cut with a hot knife into strips and bake in moderate oven (350°F) for a few minutes; then up the temperature to 400°F and bake for a further ten minutes or until browned and crisp. Separate the strips while warm.

CRACKER BALLS

¾ cup crumbled water biscuit or cream crackers
1 egg
2 Tbs. butter or rendered fat
1 tsp. chopped parsley
Grated nutmeg
Salt and black pepper
A little grated ginger root

Stir butter with the egg, add seasonings and enough crumbs so that mixture can be shaped into balls. Shape and let stand about an hour to swell; drop into boiling soup ten minutes before serving.

ALMOND DUMPLINGS

2 eggs, separated
Salt and pepper
1 tsp. parsley, chopped
¼ cup grated almonds
½ tsp. baking powder
A little flour

Beat egg yolks until light; add salt and seasoning, the baking powder and grated almonds, and add enough flour to make a stiff batter. Add beaten egg whites.

Drop the dumplings from a spoon into boiling soup ten minutes before serving.

It's a good idea to test the dumplings in a little boiling water before adding to the soup—if they fall apart, add more flour.

BAKING POWDER DUMPLINGS

½ cup flour
1 tsp. baking powder
2 Tbs. milk
Salt, pepper

Sift together dry ingredients; stir in enough milk to make a smooth batter; drop spoonfuls into boiling soup. Cover and let boil for five minutes.

SPONGE DUMPLINGS

1 egg
½ cup water or stock
½ cup flour
Salt
Grated nutmeg

Add salt and nutmeg to water and bring to boiling point; sift in the flour all at once, beating well until the mixture forms a ball and leaves the side of the pan. Cool a little, then add the egg, beating hard to keep mixture smooth. Drop by spoonfuls into boiling soup and cook for five minutes.

CRUSTY HERBED CROUTONS

4-6 slices of stale brown bread, cut into cubes
2 Tbs. butter
1 tsp. crushed thyme
Pinch of oregano
1 clove of garlic, crushed
Salt and black pepper

Melt the butter gently in a pan; add the herbs and stir well to blend; add the cubed bread, stirring to coat. Spread the cubes on a baking sheet and toast under the grill to crisp.

NOODLES AND PASTA

Making your own noodles and pasta is not as much work as you may think and the difference between what you make and what you buy is quite unbelievable. The basic recipe below is suitable for all kinds and shapes of noodles or pasta, and the finished, dried product can be kept in large covered glass jars.

BASIC PASTA DOUGH

2 cups flour (pasta or half white, half brown)
2 eggs
1 Tbs. (about) water
1 tsp. salt

Place the flour and salt in a large bowl and make a well in the centre. Drop the eggs and water into the well, and mix the dough (with your hands), adding a little more water if necessary to make a dough which is very smooth and elastic. You must knead pasta dough well—and it's as well to note that it is *not* like bread dough, for it's a lot heavier. It will need about ten minutes kneading.

Divide dough in half and cover one half with a tea towel to prevent it drying out. Now stretch and roll it out as thin as you can—it is best to try and get it translucent—and let the rolled dough stand to dry slightly.

Do the same with the other half, and by the time that it is rolled the first lot should be dried enough for cutting.

For thin noodles, sprinkle the dough with a *little* flour and gently roll up, as for a jelly roll. Slice roll thinly, shake each tangle of noodle slightly, and place on a tea towel to dry.

For broad noodles, simply cut them into one-inch-wide lengths (as long as you can make them) and dry over the back of a chair. Or, if you have a drying rack, use that.

For ravioli (stuffed pasta). For this it is best if the dough, once rolled, is cut immediately and not dried. Cut rolled dough into three-inch squares, fill with a meat, cheese, vegetable or combination of one of these stuffings (see Boreks, pp. 43-4). Fold corner of square over into triangle, press edges together with a little water and cook in boiling salted water (or in soup) for twenty minutes. They can then be served at once with a sauce, or cooked ahead of time and, just before serving, sautéed in a little butter.

BASIC PASTRY RECIPES

BASIC SHORTCRUST, (SUITABLE FOR SAVOURY DISHES)

2 cups flour
⅔ cup butter
1 tsp. salt

Rub butter into flour and salt with your fingertips until dough is like coarse sand. Pat into buttered flan dish, edging it up the sides. Prick the bottom with a fork and bake initially in a hot oven (450°F) for about ten minutes. Fill and finish baking. You may find it easier to bake the pastry 'blind' initially, i.e., by covering it with aluminium foil weighted down with dried peas or beans.

BASIC SWEET SHORTCRUST (SUITABLE FOR SWEET FILLINGS)

1 cup flour
⅓ cup sugar
½ cup butter
Pinch of salt

Sift together dry ingredients and work butter into them with fingertips as above, until dough is like coarse sand. Press into flan dish with your fingers, working it up the sides; prick the bottom. Fill and bake as below.

For a pre-baked crust place some dry beans on it.

Bake at 450°F for ten minutes, reduce heat to 350°F and bake for another fifteen minutes. If the edges threaten to darken, cover with a little foil.

FLAKY PIE CRUST FOR FRUIT PIES

2 cups flour
Good pinch of salt
¾ cup butter
6 Tbs. iced water

Sift together flour and salt and blend in the butter until pastry is like coarse sand. Sprinkle the iced water over mixture and toss until balls of dough are formed. Form dough into large ball, wrap and chill for about an hour.

Divide dough in half and roll out thinly. Line a buttered flan dish, fill with fruit, and cover with remaining dough rolled out into lid shape. Seal edges with fingers or a fork; make a few slashes across the top, brush with some milk or beaten egg yolks and bake in a moderately hot oven (400°F) for about forty-five minutes.

PUFF PASTRY

4 cups flour
2 cups butter
1 cup iced water

Have all utensils and ingredients cold.

Divide butter into three parts and pat each into a thin oblong. Place two, wrapped in napkin, into fridge and continue with the third, working it into the flour with two knives or a pastry blenders. Add some iced water, using as little of it as possible to make a smooth paste; toss paste on a floured surface, kneading it quickly into a ball-shape. Now pat it into a squarish oblong about a quarter-inch thick. Take out another butter pat from the fridge and place it on the paste. Sprinkle with a little flour and fold paste over to enclose butter, and now roll it up like a jelly roll. Pat and roll out to a quarter-inch thickness and add remaining pat of butter. Sprinkle with flour, fold paste over and roll up and pat out as before. Now fold and roll it out about four times more.

The dough will have got warm now, and soft; roll out into an oblong one last time, wrap in napkin and place in fridge. It should be very cold when you are ready to use it, and rolled out quickly. For the best puff pastry, have the dough cold and the oven hot.

BREADS

Except for the traditional Jewish Challah, I bake all breads with either all wholewheat flour or in combination with a little white flour. After all, most of the desserts are baked with white flour so it seems only right to use brown for the breads.

BASIC BROWN BREAD

1 cup boiling water (potato water is excellent)
1 cup milk, scalded
½ oz. dried yeast
2 Tbs. butter
¼ cup molasses
1 Tbs. salt
8 cups (approx.) wholewheat flour

Sprinkle the yeast on the scalded milk cooled to lukewarm (test on inside of wrist—see p. 217) to which one tablespoon of the molasses has been added. Whisk with a fork and leave to soften. Combine the water, butter and the rest of the molasses; when cooled to lukewarm, and when the yeast is frothy, combine these two, whisking together.

With a wooden spoon stir in half the flour. Then with your fingers, add and mix the rest until a workable dough is reached. Knead until smooth on a floured surface, adding more flour as necessary; place in greased bowl, cover with damp tea towel and let rise in warm place until doubled (about an hour); punch down, knead again, divide into three and shape into loaves. Bake either in loaf tins or shape into round loaves and bake in round cake tins. Cover again and let rise a second time—about thirty minutes and bake in a moderate oven (350°F) for forty-five minutes.

DARK RYE BREAD

¾ cup corn meal
1½ cups cold water
1½ cups hot water
2 Tbs. salt
2 Tbs. molasses
2 Tbs. butter
1 Tbs. caraway seed
2 cups mashed potatoes
¼ cup warm water
1½ oz. dried yeast
6 cups rye flour
2 cups wheat flour

Stir the cold water into corn meal until smooth; add hot water, caraway, and let cook, stirring constantly, for about two minutes or until it forms a mush. Take off heat, add salt, molasses and butter and let stand until lukewarm.

Dissolve the yeast in the half-cup of warm water and add this to mixture. Add mashed potatoes and finally the flours, mixing well. Turn out onto floured surface and knead until dough is smooth but stiff. Place in greased bowl, cover with tea towel and let rise in warm place until doubled.

Punch down, turn out on floured surface again, knead a little and shape into three or four rounds. Place on baking sheets or in low round cake tins which have been greased, let rise again until double and bake in a moderately hot oven (375°F) for an hour or more. Tap with knuckles and if it sounds hollow, it's done.

SOUR DOUGH FOR RYE BREAD

When making Dark Rye Bread, reserve one cup of the dough and place in a stone crock. Cover and let ferment. When baking a fresh batch of bread, use this sour dough, stirred down, in place of the yeast.

This will make a very substantial bread, delicious for cheese and other savouries.

SWEDISH RYE BREAD

1½ cups water
¼ cup dark brown sugar
3 tsp. caraway seeds
2 cups wholewheat flour
3 cups white flour
2 tsp. grated orange peel

2 Tbs. butter
2 tsp. salt
$^1/_3$ cup warm water
1 oz. dried yeast
2 cups rye flour
1 egg white, slightly beaten

Dissolve yeast in the one-third cup of warm water and whisk a little with a fork. In a saucepan, combine half a cup of the water, the brown sugar, caraway seeds, salt, and the butter. Bring to boil and simmer gently for five minutes.

Pour into a large bowl; add the remaining water (one cup) and cool mixture until lukewarm. Stir in the three cups of white flour. Now add the dissolved yeast, mix well, then stir in the wholewheat flour and the grated orange peel and continue stirring. Finally, add the rye flour, reserving about half a cup for the kneading. Turn dough onto surface on which some of the rye flour has been sprinkled and knead dough until it is smooth and like satin; use remaining rye flour if dough feels too sticky.

Form dough into ball, place in greased bowl, cover with damp tea towel and let rise in warm place until doubled—about one hour. Punch down, divide in half and shape each half into a ball. Place on lightly greased baking sheet four inches apart (or in individual cake tins with low sides), and, if desired, slash top with knife in diagonal cuts.

Cover and let rise again. Bake in hot oven (400° F) for forty-five minutes. Remove from oven, brush tops with lightly-whisked egg whites and return to oven for a couple of minutes. Take out of oven and cool on racks. This bread keeps very well and, like all rye or sour dough breads, is best eaten cold.

CHALLAH (TWISTED EGG BREAD)

8 cups white flour
2 cups hot water
2 Tbs. vegetable oil
1 Tbs. salt
1 Tbs. sugar
1 oz. dried yeast
¼ cup lukewarm water
2 eggs, beaten

Sprinkle yeast on the quarter-cup of warm water. In a large bowl, pour hot water over the salt, sugar and oil. When lukewarm, add yeast mixture, the beaten eggs and, gradually, the flour. Mix and stir, and then turn out onto floured surface and knead until smooth and elastic. Cover, set aside in warm place until doubled. Punch down, turn out and divide in half.

Each half should now be divided into four equal parts. Set one of these parts aside and roll the other three into long sausages about one-and-a-half inches thick. Make a braid, shaped as a loaf, tucking in the ends. Take the remaining part, divide it into three and make three long sausages of about half an inch thick. Braid this and place on top of larger braid. Treat other half of dough the same.

Brush both loaves with beaten egg yolk and sprinkle liberally with poppy seeds. Let rise for about fifteen minutes, then bake in a hot oven (400°F) for fifteen minutes, then turn oven down to 359°F and bake a further forty-five minutes or until loaf sounds hollow when tapped.

Eat one loaf hot but save the other and slice and toast.

PIDÉ

In Turkey they have a lovely flat bread, oblong in shape, which is sometimes used as a basis for meat dishes, sometimes simply torn into pieces and dipped into the food—very much in the same manner of chapatis.

Chapatis, I find, are very time-consuming to make and take a great deal of kneading. So I experimented until I came up with the following recipe which is quite close (if I remember rightly) to the Turkish *pidé*, and an admirable substitute for chapatis. *Pidé* can be made well in advance—I sometimes make a huge batch and use them throughout the week.

It does make it easier having a kitchen range: I simply roll the dough out to the shape of the hot plate (about seven inches by fourteen inches), flip it on, turn when it puffs, and set aside when it's been done on both sides (it looks a bit like an English muffin in texture and colour when it is cooked). But it can be done in a frying pan (without oil) over a medium heat.

1 cup warm water
1 cup milk, scalded and cooled to lukewarm
½ oz. of dry yeast
Pinch of sugar
1 tsp. salt
3 cups wholewheat flour
3 cups white flour

Sprinkle yeast on the warm milk; add sugar and whisk until frothy; when dissolved, add water, then salt, and gradually, the flour. Turn out onto very well floured surface and knead dough quickly. This dough should be very light and elastic, even a bit sticky, so don't add too much flour. Let it rise, covered, until doubled.

Punch down, divide and roll out on floured surface to about a quarter-inch thickness, flouring the rolling pin well. The shape you roll it into depends on how it is to be cooked—round if it is to be in a frying pan, long if on top of a kitchen range.

Place over the heat and, when it puffs up, turn over and brown other side; set aside to cool.

If you like, the shapes can be rolled out and then baked, but the resulting *pidé* will be very different in texture—more like a crispbread. Bake in a hot oven on greased baking sheets for about twenty minutes.

BREAKFAST CEREALS

If you think about it, it is absurd that the two most popular breakfast cereals are not only packaged and highly processed, but based on grains not grown in this country. It's even more absurd when I think back and realize that my favourite childhood breakfast was advertised as having been shot from guns. They've gone one better and now made it chocolate-flavoured to boot. My mother sent a package of the latter to my children and I am happy to say they found it horrid—we threw it to the birds and even they were suspicious at first.

I've weaned my family (and myself) from packaged

breakfast cereals by making my own muesli. Now, muesli is quite popular (it's packaged too!) and on many porridge oat packages they tell you how to make your own. What they omit to tell you is that muesli is best toasted. It takes only about twenty or thirty minutes to make enough for a family of four for a week.

TOASTED MUESLI

- 8 cups flaked grain (i.e., porridge (rolled) oats, wheat flakes or bran flakes)
- 1 cup sesame seeds
- 1 cup dessicated coconut (or more if you wish)
- 1 cup broken nuts (optional)
- ½ cup honey
- ½ cup vegetable oil
- 1-2 cups currants, sultanas or raisins

In a large baking dish (a thoroughly clean roasting pan will do) place the flaked grain and bake in a hot oven (400°F) for about five minutes, or until just beginning to brown slightly. Take out and now add the coconut, sesame seeds and any nuts (or sunflower seeds) you wish to add. Mix thoroughly and return to oven for an additional five minutes.

Take out one last time, and pour over it the honey and oil which has been slightly warm and mixed. Stir the mixture well to coat everything with the oil and honey mixture; return to the oven and bake a further five minutes. Take out, cool, add raisins, currants or sultanas, and store in glass jars (we use old sweet jars).

The above muesli can also be made on top of the stove in a large, clean skillet. Halve all the ingredients and proceed as above, toasting in the skillet rather than in the oven.

Incidentally, we find that the above muesli is best if mixed with some plain porridge oats. As it is, we use it for snacks, the younger ones taking it to school for their 'piece'. For breakfast, we make it half and half—half muesli, half plain oats. Chop in some apples and simply add milk--no sugar is necessary.

WHEAT PORRIDGE

For a change from oat porridge on cold mornings, simply take some pre-cooked wheat, place in saucepan with equal amounts of water and milk, and heat through gently. Serve with a pat of butter, some brown sugar (or honey) and fresh milk. Also good with a pinch of cinnamon or a little grated nutmeg on top. (Rye can be treated in the same way and has a nuttier taste.)

BREAKFAST PANCAKES

Sunday mornings are the perfect time for late, heavy breakfasts and the following pancakes are one of our favourite special breakfasts.

- 1 egg beaten
- 1¼ cups soured milk (milk with a little vinegar)
- 2 Tbs. vegetable oil
- 1½ cups wholewheat flour
- 1 tsp. baking powder
- 1 tsp. sugar
- ½ tsp. soda
- Pinch of salt

Mix all the liquid ingredients together with a whisk. Combine the dry ingredients, sifted, in a bowl. Add the liquid to the dry and whisk thoroughly until smooth; the batter will be quite thin.

Heat butter in skillet, and ladle out about half a teacupful for each pancake; when bubbles appear, and burst, turn the pancake and brown on other side. There should be enough for about sixteen four-inch pancakes.

Serve with butter, honey, chopped apples, jam, marmalade, or anything you fancy.

DAIRY PRODUCTS

We've never kept cows so I can't speak with any authority on cow's milk products. Of course, the making of Crowdie (soft cheese) and sour cream is the same for both goats and cows so the directions for those products are given with full confidence. I would suggest that anyone with cow's milk to spare, and interested in making cheese, get hold of a copy of *Farmhouse Fare* (particulars in the Bibliography at back of the book) and read the chapter on cheese-making.

But, in case you can't get hold of a copy, and would like to try making cheese, simply, below is a recipe given to me by a friend who made cheese regularly last spring and summer from the milk of their cow.

SIMPLE COW'S CHEESE—MEDIUM HARD

Put seven pints skimmed milk (reserve the cream, or 'top', for cream) in a warm place to go quite solid. This will take two to three days, depending on the weather (incidentally, sultry thundery weather is best for this). When solid, gently pour into a saucepan, cover, and heat very gently, without stirring, on the lowest possible heat, until the curd sinks slightly, leaving a clear whey. This will take about twenty minutes. Now gently, drain the curd through a cloth (muslin or cheesecloth) and add salt to taste.

Add chopped chives (or a little rubbed sage, dillweed or parsley) and press into a cake tin in which holes have been punched on the sides and the bottom, and the whole lined with clean muslin. Cover with a piece of muslin, a flat wooden disc or plate, and put on a three-pound weight; after a few hours, increase weight to seven pounds. Next day, take cheese out, turn, place in tin a clean cloth, and put cheese in, replacing weights. Do this for three days then take out and place on a board and turn occasionally, keeping it in a cool place. Will keep about three weeks.

Cake tins make admirable cheese moulds but remember when punching in the holes to make them from the inside-out so that there are no rough edges to catch on the cloth on the inside. Also, when the cheese is in the mould, place it on a bowl over which have been placed a couple of sticks and rest the mould (cake tin) on the sticks so that excess whey will drip into the bowl.

CROWDIE

For Crowdie you can follow the above recipe until the curd is drained through cloth. This drained curd is the Crowdie and, if you wish to use it for sweet Cheese Pies (pp. 64-5) add only a very small amount of salt. If on the other hand you wish it for savoury dishes or simply to spread on bread, add salt, pepper, and any desired chopped herb. A little garlic pressed into the cheese is extremely good. Also, one neighbour creams her Crowdie with a little butter for a richer consistency.

Crowdie does not have to be made with skimmed milk, however, unless you want to save the cream for dessert making. Goat's milk is not so easily skimmed as cow's but in the late spring and summer, when the goats are eating plenty of green grass, their milk separates more easily so that, at one go, I can make sour cream and Crowdie.

In low pans I pour the milk to be left to sour; I add to the pans at each milking and leave in a warm place, as in the above recipe. In about three days, the cream will have risen to the top in a thick smooth coat. I skim this off with a wooden spatula in which holes have been drilled, and place this sour cream in a cool place to use as required. The rest of the milk can now be treated as above for Crowdie—either sweet or savoury.

FETA GOAT'S CHEESE (WITHOUT CHEESE RENNET)

Feta is really only a semi-hard, salty Crowdie type of cheese and is made very much as above.

Take half a gallon of milk (or whatever quantity you wish, but it is as well to make a lot of this as it will keep), and set in a warm place to go solid, as in the cows' cheese recipe. Now heat (again as in above recipe) until curd leaves the sides of the pan and sinks slightly, leaving a clear whey. With a knife cut the curd into wedges and add about a scant tablespoon of salt.

Let rest for a few minutes, and now carefully ladle the curd and pack into a lined tin. Place about four pounds of weight on top and leave for three hours; then turn and place weight on top again. The next day take out of mould, replace cloth with clean cloth, salt the cheese and replace, weighing down. Keep in the mould for about three to four days, turning each day.

To keep this cheese (which should slice in thick slices but tends to crumble into largish pieces) submerge in a brine solution (one cup salt to five cups water).

If I sound a little vague about the consistency of feta, it is because it does vary. If you like it harder, then you must increase the weights.

FETA GOAT'S CHEESE WITH RENNET

To make this cheese use fresh milk. (If you have a fridge large enough to store the milk, or a cool place, keep the milk from three or four consecutive milkings.) For every gallon of milk (well mixed if using consecutive milkings) add half a teaspoon of rennet, well mixed with some of the milk, and stirred into the milk when heated or just under blood temperature. (It will feel slightly cool on your wrist).

Place the milk over a very gentle heat and warm until it is just a little above blood temperature (feeling a little warm on your wrist). Cover and let curd form in a warm place (takes about an hour).

Now cut the curd into wedges with a knife and sprinkle about two tablespoons of salt over all. Let sit a while longer in warm place, covered, and then pack into moulds as above.

Place a seven-pound weight on and leave for a half hour. Turn, replace weight for about two or three hours. Turn, change muslin cloth, salt, and return to mould with ten pounds weight. The next day turn in mould and replace weight. After fourth day it can come out of the mould. It will be slightly harder than above feta but be kept in brine the same way.

GOAT'S CHEESE—HARD

This cheese is made as the recipe above, but instead of

increasing weight to ten pounds, the weight should be increased to about twenty pounds. Incidentally, the thinner the cheese, the less weights you will need for less time. So it is really best to experiment and see what suits your own kitchen.

When the cheese comes out of the mould, leave in a cool place, on a piece of well-salted straw matting, and turn occasionally. This should be done for about a week. It can be eaten now, but can also be kept in which case you must do the following: rub each cheese with oil and a little paprika, rubbing the oil into the cheese well. Leave to stand for three days, then repeat the process. Leave for another three days and repeat process again. Leave for a week, repeat oiling. Leave for two weeks, and the cheese can then be stored and kept all through the winter.

Cheese can also be submerged in oil for keeping but that seems a little expensive!

YOGHURT

Yoghurt has been around for hundreds of years so it seems a little ridiculous to invest in a fancy yoghurt-making device to make a simple process more complicated.

For every pint of milk you use, you will need one tablespoon of yoghurt. It is worth trying to get hold of the real thing from a health food store rather than the bland supermarket variety.

Pour milk into saucepan and heat it up; when it starts to rise up the sides of the pan, take off heat and cool down to blood temperature (test on inside of wrist; if you feel nothing, the milk's at the right temperature). Whisk some of this milk into the yoghurt, then whisk the yoghurt and milk into the rest of the milk. Put it in a ceramic dish, cover, wrap in a thick towel and place for at least eight hours in an airing cupboard or somewhere warm, away from draughts. A peasant family in Greece would take their yoghurt, carefully wrapped in a blanket, and stick it in the foot of the bed with them for the night. So, if you don't have an airing cupboard, take it to bed with you!

Cool it and you will find it will firm more; save some for your next batch and just keep on going like that.

SPROUTING SEEDS

Sprouting seeds is extremely simple and the results are delicious on their own in a salad, or as an addition to any vegetable dish. It's the closest to instant pure vegetable that we can have, and the protein content is always high.

For the larger grains and beans, you will have to soak them so that they will sprout easily.

- 1/3 cup groats, wheat, barley or tic beans, soaked for 24 hours
- 1 large coffee jar
- Piece of cheesecloth, muslin, or fine mesh netting to fit over the top
- Elastic band to secure cloth

Place your grains in coffee jar and fill with water; secure cloth on top with elastic band and shake contents thoroughly.

Tip out the water and leave the bottle on its side in a warm place. Repeat this process morning and night for about four to six days, by which time the sprouts will be about one to two inches long.

For smaller seeds (mung beans, alfalfa, fenugreek, or even mustard and cress) the seeds do not have to be soaked beforehand. Use a quarter-cup of seeds per coffee jar with cloth and elastic band. Place seeds in jar, cover with water, secure cloth and shake vigorously; pour water out. Repeat this about three times, then leave the beans on their side in a warm place as above.

If you like sprouts to be green, place in direct sunlight for the last day; we usually sprout ours in a cupboard adjacent to our kitchen range where it is both warm and dark.

HOME-MADE WINES

Home winemaking can offer a delicious, cheap and thoroughly ecological way to savour the countryside. Basically, all that is required in the way of facilities and equipment is a warm place in which to produce the fermentation—an airing cupboard, or a shelf, or floor space by a kitchen range, radiator or hot-water tank will do fine. (An even heat is best but a drop in temperature for part of the day will merely slow and not kill the fermentation.) You will also need a fermentation vessel, together with a straining cloth, a piece of plastic tube for syphoning, bottles, corks and ancillary kitchen equipment of the usual kind (jugs, a wooden spoon, etc.).

The most essential ingredients in wine, apart from water, are yeast and sugar in some form or other. Yeast, when introduced to a glucose/fructose solution, converts sugar into carbon dioxide and alcohol. Other important ingredients are flavourings, usually imparted by fruits, herbs or flowers; the nutrient salts for yeast that have to be introduced in small quantities to some fermenting liquors; fruit acids and finally tannin, though the latter affects only the finished wine and not the fermentation process itself. Acids are present to a varying degree in all fruits and tannin is present in the skins of many and also in tea. Like various wine yeasts, nutrient salts, citric acid and grape tannin may be bought in the winemaking department of chemists.

That part of the winemaking process in which carbon dioxide is given off and alcohol produced, called fermentation, usually takes between one and four months (very occasionally up to six), depending mostly on the original quantity of sugar present. However, as the alcohol level in a wine approaches eighteen per cent by volume or thirty degrees proof (commercial wines above this level are necessarily fortified) the yeast is inhibited by the alcohol already present and fermentation slows ever increasingly, and finally ceases. So putting excess sugar in your wine liquor will simply make a sweet wine, not an over-strong one.

On the other hand, wine *can* be drunk 'young' once the fermentation has ceased, when it will be almost clear, and a very young though weaker wine can be made by using less sugar than the quantity given, if you can't wait! Wines do improve with keeping though, and you should try and be patient with a bottled wine for at least a year. Generally we double up on a winemaking recipe and drink half 'young'—or use it for cooking, for which it can be original and excellent—and bottle the remaining half for maturing.

It is essential to keep a fermenting wine covered, especially denying access to the vinegar fly, which may turn it to vinegar! (Let him in, however, if you want culinary vinegar of a highly original variety, or add a little commercial vinegar near the end of the fermentation process.) On the other hand, the carbon dioxide must be allowed to escape from a fermenting wine, and for this reason the type of fermentation vessel most favoured by home winemakers is a one-gallon glass jar fitted with a small fermentation 'trap' or valve fitted into a cork bung—all of which can be bought cheaply at a chemist's. But since some kind of plastic bucket or container with a wide top will also be needed, in most cases, to soak the flowers or fruit used, you may prefer simply to acquire a one- or two-gallon plastic bucket with a close-fitting lid to begin with. The lid can be bored with quarter- to half-inch holes in a couple of places and the holes plugged with cotton wool, which should allow the gasses to escape without admitting the dreaded vinegar fly! For your first attempt you could even make do with an open bowl or plastic bucket with a cloth tied closely across the top.

BASIC FRUIT WINE

To make a dry wine it is important never to use more than about 3½ lb. sugar—at the most 3¾ lb. However, since most fruits contain a small to moderate amount of sugar of their own, the sugar content of a dry fruit wine has to be reduced in some cases. Generally, for almost sugarless fruits—elderberries, sloes, rosehips, rowanberries, green gooseberries etc.—use 3½ lb. sugar for a strong dry wine. For fruits that are sweeter—bananas, peaches, apples, pears, ripe strawberries etc.—cut the quantity of sugar by ½ lb. or, in the case of citrus fruits, 4 oz.

Many wines, e.g. apple, pear, strawberry, peach, etc., are improved by the addition of extra fruit, if you can spare it. In this case reduce the sugar content by 2 oz. for each extra 1 lb. of fruit above 4 lb.

Do not use acid or bitter fruits such as sloes or rowanberries to excess, or elderberries, of which you should not use more than 3 lb. to the gallon, because of their high tannin content. This latter feature does, however, make them a good addition to other wine liquors in moderation.

- 4 lb. fruit (almost any, wild or domestic, will do—except tomatoes!)
- 3-3½ lb. sugar
- 1 tsp. wine yeast, or brewer's yeast if unavailable
- 1 gallon water

Optional

- ½ lb. barley (for extra 'body' in thin wines)
- 2 tsp. citric acid or juice of 2 lemons and 2 oranges (important in low-acid wines, e.g., banana, strawberry)
- 1 tsp. grape tannin, or 1 heaped Tbs. tea (improves all except elderberry, apple, pear, sloe, damson, plum and grape wines)
- 1 tsp. wine nutrient salts (if omitted, watch fermentation for premature end)

Wash or rinse fruit well and cut into pieces, stoning plums, cherries, peaches etc., but do not peel any fruit except bananas (which should be fermented in a muslin bag in liquor). Fruit skins impart tannin and colour to a wine.

Mash fruit in a bucket or large bowl and add half the sugar and, if used, the crushed barley, fruit juice (or acid) and tea or tannin. Boil the gallon of water and pour over the mash. Stir well to dissolve sugar and when the liquor has cooled to about 70°F dissolve the yeast and nutrient, if used, in a little of the juice, and return to the bulk.

Keep covered lightly and let stand in a warm place for three or four days, stirring daily. A brisk fermentation should result. Strain through muslin, a nylon bag or loosely-woven cotton cloth onto remainder of sugar. Dissolve sugar and press or squeeze as much liquor as possible from the pulp remainder before straining again into fermentation vessel.

Fit fermentation vessel with a trap or cover and store in a warm place (65°–75°F is best) until it is almost clear and fermentation has ceased.

Syphon wine off sediment with a plastic tube. (If fermentation takes longer than a couple of months and brewer's yeast has been used, syphoning-off should be done at two monthly intervals, returning wine to vessel, to avoid a yeasty taste.)

Wine may now either be drunk 'young', bottled (in which case there will be a very slight sediment in the bottles which will not affect the taste of the wine or, if carefully poured, the clarity) or returned to the fermenting vessel for another three months or so until absolutely clear before bottling. In this case there will be no sediment at all in the bottles—provided that wine is syphoned into bottles, of course.

Bottles should be stored on their sides in a cool place. If retaining wine in larger vessel for a second three-month period for complete clearing, as above, the temperature can also be cooler. Wine only needs warmth for the primary fermentation.

Note, too, that red wines—elderberry, raspberry, blackberry, cherry etc. should be fermented in dark vessels and bottled in dark bottles. Alternatively, the bottles and fermentation vessels should be kept in a dark place or covered with cloth or brown paper, if the glorious colour of the wine is to be retained.

TEA AND SULTANA SHERRY

Leftover tea makes an excellent sherry, particularly if you take herbal teas sometimes or use fragrant China teas. The following recipe is perfect for winter months when fruits are not around—and it will use up all your leftover tea in the process! With very little trouble you should produce a delicious medium-dry sherry.

2 gallons strained tea 'leftovers' (no milk please!)
6 lb. raisins, sultanas, currents or mixed dried fruit
2 tsp. citric acid, or juice of 6 lemons
2 level tsp. yeast nutrient salts
4 lb. granulated sugar
1 tsp. wine yeast (preferably sherry)

This will make two gallons of wine, but if your fermentation container (bucket or bowl) is smaller, reduce quantities accordingly.

Save tea from pot, straining into a jar or your fermentation container. Keep covered in a cool place. When you have four pints, mince half the sultanas or dried fruits (3 lb.), put into fermentation vessel with tea and introduce yeast. Cover with cloth or lid with cotton-wool-plugged vents, and keep in a warm place (about 70°F).

Fermentation will begin on the sugar in the raisins or sultanas. Continue to add tea, stirring at least daily as you do so, until you have one gallon, and then add the remainder of the dried fruits, minced well, and all the remaining ingredients except the sugar.

Continue stirring and adding tea to 1½ gallons, then add 1 lb. of the sugar. Add another 1 lb. at about the 1¾-gallon stage (the important thing is to keep a sturdy fermentation going continuously). When a full two gallons of tea have been chalked up (keep a tally on lid or paper—a measuring jug is essential, of course) strain the fermenting liquor off the pulp twice, as in the previous recipe. Add the remaining 2 lb. sugar, stir in well and ferment the liquor right out, as before. Bottle if possible!

If your container is not quite big enough for two gallons of tea and the dried fruit as well (and it will keep rising) strain the pulp off at the 1½- or 1¾-gallon stage, making sure, though, that the sugar in the dried fruit has had a chance to ferment right out. Then add the remaining tea and sugar in stages.

Herbal and Flower Wines

A variant of the above recipe is to make your wine of an infusion of flowers and/or herbs from the outset, using dried fruit or minced barley, if you like, to give 'body'. Dandelion heads make a particularly delicious wine or sherry and elderflower wine is also well known among amateur winemakers.

Other flowers often put to use include marigolds, honeysuckle, hawthorn blossom and meadowsweet. Most common garden herbs can also be used for wines, including fennel and rue (traditional ingredients of sack), parsley, lemon balm, hyssop, sage, etc. As for teas, the best rule is to experiment with your own combinations.

The following flower wine recipe can be used as a basis, though it is worth remembering that pungent herbs should be used more sparingly than blander flower heads!

2-3 qt. flower heads (4 qt. meadowsweet, if used)
3½ lb. sugar
1 gallon water
2 oranges and 2 lemons, or 2 tsp. citric acid
Yeast, yeast nutrient
1 heaped Tbs. tea, or 1 tsp. grape tannin

Optional

1-4 lb. minced dried fruit

If using dried fruit, reduce sugar content by half a pound for every one pound of dried fruit. Note, though, that dandelion wine almost demands to be well-bodied!

Pick the flowers while open on a dry, sunny day. (If using garden herbs the same rule applies.) Pour the boiling water over the flower heads, tea, grated rind of citrus fruits and minced dried fruits (if used) and sugar. When cooled to about 70°F add yeast and nutrient and fruit juice or acid. Ferment for ten days on the pulp in a covered bowl or bucket. Strain well as before, transfer to fermenting vessel and ferment out and bottle as usual.

BEANS
WHEAT
RELISH

Bibliography

Collins Guide to Mushrooms and Toadstools, Morton Lange and F. Bayard Hora, Collins, 1963

Companion Plants, Helen Philbrick and Richard B. Gregg, Watkins, 1967

Concise British Flora in Colour, Martin W. Keble, Michael Joseph, 1969

Farmhouse Fare, Countrywise Books, 1966

First Steps in Winemaking, C. J. J. Berry, Amateur Winemaker, 1968

Food for Free, Richard Mabey, Collins, 1972

Index